Appeal
FAVOURITES

[165 recipes from the pages of *Appeal* magazine]

Our sincerest thanks to all the food experts who contributed their recipes to this volume: Patricia Chuey, Joanne Facchin, Nathan Fong, Laura Kalina, Heather McColl, Irene McGuinness, Jan Peskett, Sharon Schmidt, Jennifer Stamper, Becky Paris Turner

Canada Wide Magazines & Communications Ltd.
4th Floor, 4180 Lougheed Highway
Burnaby, British Columbia V5C 6A7 Canada
Tel. 604-299-7311 Fax 604-299-9188

Library and Archives Canada Cataloguing in Publication

Main entry under title:
Appeal Favourites

Includes index.
ISBN 0-9697585-6-1

LIBRARY AND ARCHIVES CANADA CATALOGUING IN PUBLICATION

Appeal favourites/editor, Kim Mah.
Includes recipes originally published in Appeal magazine.

Includes index.
ISBN 0-9697585-6-1

1. Cookery.   I. Mah, Kim, 1964-
TX714.A64 2005   641.5   C2005-905049-7

Edited by Kim Mah
Book design by Anya Lewis
Typeset by Ina Bowerbank
Cover photo by Raeff Miles (recipe: Fiery Prawn Wok, page 105)
Photo art direction by Cathy Mullaly
Printed and bound in Canada by Kromar Printing

[contents]

[appetizers & beverages]

Hot and Classy Artichoke Crab Dip
Crisp Parmesan and Garlic Pita Toasts
Pizza Packets
Phyllo Sausage Rolls
Cocktail Ham Balls
Rolled Roasted Bell Peppers with Yogurt Dip
Light Stuffed Jalapeño Poppers
Elegant Camembert with Cranberry Chutney
Mushroom Tapas with Pork and Pine Nuts
Goat Cheese with Green Olive Tapenade
Baked Crab Wontons
Spring Vegetable Terrine
Mini Turkey Empanadas
Pink Grapefruit Mimosas
Frosted Coffee and Chocolate Punch
Pineapple Tea
Spicy Virgin Caesar
Watermelon Berry Virgin Margarita
Winter Marsala Chai
Apple Blackcurrant Cider

hot and classy artichoke crab dip

MAKES 2-1/2 C. [625 ML]

1	Tbsp. [15 mL] unsalted butter
1	cup [250 mL] finely minced onion
3	garlic cloves, minced
2	Tbsp. [30 mL] all-purpose flour
1	cup [250 mL] low-salt chicken broth
1/2	cup [125 mL] 1% milk
4	oz. [125 g] light cream cheese, cubed
1	[14 fl. oz./398 mL] tin artichoke hearts, drained and chopped
1	[120 g] tin crabmeat, drained
1	tsp. [5 mL] minced fresh dill
1/4	tsp. [2 mL] each salt and freshly ground white pepper
1/4	tsp. [2 mL] finely grated fresh lemon peel
	Dash of hot sauce [optional]

*Calories: 54;
Protein 5.1 g;
Carbohydrate 2.7 g;
Fibre 0.2 g;
Fat 2.4 g/1 Tbsp.
[15 mL] dip*

1. Melt butter in a heavy-bottomed saucepan. Add onion and garlic and sauté over medium-low heat until onion is soft, about 6 minutes. Be careful not to brown.

2. Sprinkle with flour and stir for 2 minutes. It will become dry and crumbly.

3. Gradually stir in broth and milk. Bring to a boil, stirring constantly. Reduce heat to low and continue to cook until mixture thickens, stirring frequently, about 2 minutes.

4. Stir in cream cheese and continue to stir until cheese cubes dissolve.

5. Fold in chopped artichokes, crabmeat, seasonings and lemon peel. Add hot sauce if you wish.

6. To serve, gently stir in a heavy-bottomed saucepan over low heat until bubbly and piping hot. Transfer to a medium-size ceramic serving dish and serve warm.

Serving suggestion: Serve with toast points and Belgian endive leaves for dipping.

PHOTO: TONY HURLEY

crisp parmesan and garlic pita toasts

MAKES 8 SERVINGS

1	pkg. pita bread [6"/15 cm rounds]
1/2	cup [125 mL] extra virgin olive oil
3	garlic cloves, minced
1	tsp. [5 mL] dried oregano
1	cup [250 mL] freshly grated Parmesan cheese

1. Preheat oven to 350°F [180°C].

2. Using a sharp knife, cut each pita round into 6 triangles. Separate each piece into 2 halves. Place pieces on a baking sheet with baked side facing up.

3. In a small bowl, mix together olive oil, garlic and oregano.

4. Brush each pita triangle with oil mixture; sprinkle Parmesan on each piece. Bake until golden and crisp, about 5-7 minutes.

5. Remove from oven; allow to cool. Store in an airtight container. Delicious served with a variety of dips.

Calories: 431;
Protein 14 g;
Carbohydrate 51 g;
Fibre 0.8 g;
Fat 19 g/serving

pizza packets

MAKES 39 PACKETS

1/2	lb. [250 g] pizza salami, diced very small
1/2	lb. [250 g] Swiss Gruyère cheese, diced very small
1	[114 mL] tin sliced black olives, drained
2	tsp. [10 mL] dried oregano leaves, crushed
1-1/2	tsp. [8 mL] coarse black pepper
3	roma tomatoes, seeded, diced
13	sheets phyllo pastry, thawed
	Melted butter

Calories: 108;
Protein 4 g;
Carbohydrate 5 g;
Fibre 0.2 g;
Fat 8 g/packet

1. Combine first 6 ingredients in a medium bowl; mix well.

2. Preheat oven to 400°F [200°C].

3. Melt butter in a small custard cup; select a brush and a sharp knife before you start.

4. When all items are ready, unwrap the phyllo pastry. Take out the 13 needed sheets. Roll others and return to box and to the freezer or refrigerator. Keep the 13 you are using under a damp cloth while you work.

5. Place one sheet on counter vertical to you. Use a sharp knife to make two cuts from top to bottom of the sheet, leaving you with three long strips of pastry about 3" x 15" [7.5 x 37.5 cm]. Brush very lightly with melted butter.

6. Place a heaping Tbsp. [15 mL] of meat and cheese filling at the bottom of each strip of pastry. Lift bottom left corner of first strip over filling to the right so you have a triangle parcel started, with the right edges lined up. Now take the bottom right corner [2 layers now] and fold the parcel up, keeping the right sides lined up. Now fold the parcel from the right to the left side of the strip, keeping the left sides lined up. Continue folding first right, then left up the pastry strip to the end; you should have a triangle-shaped packet with filling inside.

7. Place on an ungreased baking tray with the end flap underneath.

8. Repeat with the other two strips of pastry. Repeat the process with all 13 sheets of phyllo. You should now have 13 x 3 packets = 39 in total. The melted butter you first brush each strip with should hold the packets together, especially if you remember to place the end flap down on the baking tray.

9. Brush the outside of each packet with melted butter.

10. Bake about 10 minutes or until golden brown. Serve at once.

Note: Uncooked packets freeze well; thaw before baking as above. They may also be frozen after baking and can be reheated in a 350°F [180°C] oven about 10 minutes or until crisped again.

phyllo sausage rolls

MAKES 36 ROLLS

2	lbs. [1 kg] pork sausages
1/2	cup [125 mL] fine dry bread crumbs
3/4	cup [175 mL] chopped parsley
3-4	Tbsp. [45-60 mL] chopped fresh sage
5	garlic cloves, minced
1	tsp. [5 mL] crushed red pepper flakes
2	Tbsp. [30 mL] Worcestershire sauce
1/2	tsp. [3 mL] coarse black pepper
6	sheets phyllo pastry, thawed
3	Tbsp. [45 mL] melted butter

1. Squeeze meat out of sausages; combine with next 7 ingredients in a large bowl. Mix well with your hands until totally combined.

2. Place first sheet of phyllo pastry horizontally on the counter. [Keep all other sheets under a damp cloth so they do not dry out while you work.] Lightly brush with melted butter. Place second sheet on top. Lightly brush 2/3 of this sheet, leaving the 1/3 closest to you unbuttered.

3. Place 1/3 of the sausage mixture in a long line along the edge of the pastry edge closest to you. Roll up away from you like a jelly roll. Use both hands to "slim" and even the roll, trimming the ends with a sharp knife.

4. Cut the roll in half, then in half again. Cut each piece into three, making 12 sausage rolls.

5. Place on ungreased baking tray. Repeat twice more with two sheets of phyllo each time and 1/3 of the sausage mixture. You should now have 36 rolls.

6. Lightly brush tops of rolls with remaining melted butter. Place in refrigerator until ready to bake. [The rolls will last in the fridge up to 1 day. You may also wrap the rolls at this point and freeze until you need them. Do not brush tops with butter before freezing.]

7. Preheat oven to 425°F [220°C]. [If using thawed rolls, brush tops with melted butter before baking.] Bake rolls about 15-18 minutes or until well browned. Serve warm.

Note: You may use half a 397 g package of frozen puff pastry instead of phyllo. Roll out to a horizontal rectangle about 15" x 12" [37.5 x 30 cm]. Cut horizontally into 3 equal pieces, each 15" x 4" [37.5 x 10 cm]. Lay 1/3 of sausage mixture down the centre of each piece. Brush a little water around the pastry edges; bring pastry up around each line of meat and roll back and forth until you have a long slim roll. Cut as described above into 36 rolls. Similarly, regular pie pastry may be used. Rolls may be frozen raw or baked – with any of the three types of pastry. For best results, freeze raw. Thaw rolls before cooking; to reheat cooked rolls, place in 350°F [180°C] oven for about 10 minutes.

Calories: 158;
Protein 4 g;
Carbohydrate 4 g;
Fibre 0.1 g;
Fat 14 g/roll [phyllo
pastry version]

cocktail ham balls

MAKES 6 DOZEN

1	lb. [500 g] ground ham
1-1/4	lbs. [625 g] ground pork
3/4	cup [175 mL] ground soda crackers [about 2-1/2 oz./75 g]
3/4	cup [175 mL] ground Ritz crackers [about 2-1/2 oz./75 g]
2	eggs, beaten
3/4	cup [175 mL] low-fat evaporated milk
1/4	tsp. [2 mL] coarse black pepper
1/4	tsp. [2 mL] salt
1-1/8	cups [280 mL] packed brown sugar
1	tsp. [5 mL] dry English mustard
6	Tbsp. [90 mL] white vinegar
6	Tbsp. [90 mL] water

Calories: 72;
Protein 4 g;
Carbohydrate 5 g;
Fibre 0 g;
Fat 4 g/ball

1. Preheat oven to 275°F [140°C].

2. Combine first 8 ingredients in a large bowl; mix well with your hands until totally combined.

3. Make 6 dozen tiny balls; place in one or two layers in a sprayed or lightly greased large shallow baker.

4. Combine last 3 ingredients in a small bowl; mix well and pour over balls in baker. Cover tightly and place in centre of oven. Bake about 1 hour.

5. Remove cover, carefully turn balls in sauce. Bake again, uncovered, about 1-1/2 hours, stirring and turning in sauce several times. Sauce will eventually become thick and very sticky, coating the balls.

6. Remove from oven; let stand 5 minutes; turn again to coat in thickening sauce. Serve at once with toothpicks and plenty of napkins!

PHOTO: JOE BORRELLI

rolled roasted bell peppers with yogurt dip

MAKES 6 SERVINGS

Tapenade:

1/2	cup [125 mL] pitted black olives
6	anchovy fillets
3	Tbsp. [45 mL] drained capers
4	garlic cloves, peeled
1/4	cup [60 mL] olive oil
	Black pepper

Peppers:

8	small red or yellow bell peppers
1/3	lb. [165 g] Feta cheese, crumbled
	Flat-leafed parsley leaves

Dip:

1/2	cup [125 mL] plain low-fat yogurt
1	Tbsp. [15 mL] minced fresh mint
2	tsp. [10 mL] fresh lemon juice
	Fresh ground black pepper

1. Combine all tapenade ingredients in a food processor or in a beaker with a hand-held blender. Process until you have a coarse but well-combined mixture. [This can be kept in the refrigerator for up to 3 days.] Preheat broiler.

2. Cut peppers into quarters, scooping out the seeds and inner pith and core.

3. Place pieces, skin side up, on a baking sheet. Broil until totally black.

4. Place in a paper bag until cool. Pull off blackened skin and lay roasted pepper pieces on the counter, inside up.

5. Spread each piece with some of the tapenade. Top each with some cheese and a parsley leaf. Roll up tightly and secure with a toothpick.

6. Place rolls on a serving platter and cover with plastic wrap until serving time.

7. To make the dip, combine remaining ingredients, mixing well. Place in a small bowl with the platter. Pass the dip along with the pepper rolls while offering drinks before dinner.

*Calories: 261;
Protein 9 g;
Carbohydrate 18 g;
Fibre 4.5 g;
Fat 17 g/serving*

appetizer

light stuffed jalapeño poppers

MAKES 16 APPETIZERS

2	tsp. [10 mL] vegetable oil
3	Tbsp. [45 mL] finely minced red onion
3	garlic cloves, minced
4	oz. [125 g] spreadable light cream cheese, at room temperature
2	Tbsp. [30 mL] finely grated fresh Parmesan cheese
1/8	tsp. [1 mL] salt
8	Jalapeño peppers
4	egg whites
1	cup [250 mL] fine dry toasted bread crumbs
1/2	cup [125 mL] prepared salsa [hot, medium or mild]
	All-purpose canola cooking spray
	Freshly ground black pepper to taste

Calories: 61;
Protein 3.1 g;
Carbohydrate 7.1 g;
Fibre 0.6 g;
Fat 2.5 g/popper

1. Heat oil in a small frying pan.
2. Add onion and garlic and sauté until soft, about 5 minutes. Do not brown.
3. Transfer to a small bowl and add cream cheese, Parmesan, salt and pepper. Stir to blend. Set aside.
4. Wearing rubber gloves, cut peppers in half, lengthwise. Using a small spoon, scrape the inside membranes and seeds out.
5. Fill pepper halves with cheese mixture and spread the surface with a palette knife until smooth. Peppers can be made to this point, covered and refrigerated overnight.
6. Preheat oven to 350°F [180°C].
7. Line a 12" x 15" [30 x 38 cm] baking sheet with parchment paper.
8. Whisk egg whites in a bowl until frothy.
9. Place bread crumbs in a separate shallow bowl.
10. Dip pepper halves, one at a time, in the egg whites and then dip into bread crumbs until evenly coated all over.
11. Place coated pepper halves in a single layer, cut side up, on prepared baking sheet. Lightly spray with canola cooking spray.
12. Bake about 20 minutes or until crisp and golden. Serve immediately with 1/2 tsp. [3 mL] salsa spooned on top.

light
stuffed
jalapeño
poppers

elegant
camembert
with
cranberry
chutney

elegant camembert with cranberry chutney

MAKES 6 SERVINGS

1	[6 oz./200 g] round of fresh Camembert*
1/2	cup [125 mL] prepared cranberry chutney**
1/4	cup [60 mL] pecans, toasted, chopped
	Fresh cranberries, figs, Medjool dates and kumquats [optional]
	Water crackers

*For firmness, choose a young Camembert.
**You may substitute an alternative fruity chutney.

---

1. Slice Camembert in half horizontally and separate.

2. Spread chutney on bottom half. Sprinkle with toasted pecans. Cover with top half of cheese.

3. Just before microwaving, garnish serving platter with fresh cranberries, kumquats, sliced figs and dates, leaving a space for the Camembert.

4. When ready to serve, place cheese in a microwave-safe dish and microwave uncovered, on medium power for 1-2 minutes, or just until cheese begins to soften slightly. [Time will vary depending on your microwave.] Do not overheat or it will become runny.

5. Remove to the garnished serving platter.

Serving suggestion: Top Camembert with a sprig of holly or cranberry, or parsley sprigs, and serve with crackers for dipping.

Calories: 135;
Protein 7.2 g;
Carbohydrate 2 g;
Fibre 0.6 g;
Fat 11.2 g/serving

mushroom tapas with pork and pine nuts

MAKES ABOUT 20 TAPAS

1	lb. [500 g] large white mushrooms, about 20
	Juice of 1 lemon
1	Tbsp. [15 mL] unsalted butter
1/2	small onion, finely minced [about 3 Tbsp./45 mL]
1	garlic clove, finely minced
4	oz. [125 g] lean ground pork
1/4	tsp. [2 mL] ground cumin
1/4	cup [60 mL] crumbled Chèvre [goat cheese] or 1/2 [4 oz./125 g] pkg. plain low-fat cream cheese
2	Tbsp. [30 mL] pine nuts, toasted
2	Tbsp. [30 mL] minced fresh parsley
1/4	tsp. [2 mL] Spanish-style paprika
	Salt and freshly ground black pepper

*Calories: 45;
Protein 2.5 g;
Carbohydrate 1.5 g;
Fibre 0.5 g;
Fat 3.5 g/mushroom
cap*

1. Separate the stems from the caps of each mushroom and finely mince the stems. You should have about 1/2 cup [125 mL]. Reserve.

2. Brush inside of mushroom caps with a little lemon juice to prevent them from discolouring while preparing filling.

3. Melt butter in a large skillet. Add onion and garlic and sauté over medium-low heat until softened and onion is translucent, about 7 minutes.

4. Increase heat to medium. Add ground pork and mushroom stems and stir-fry until meat is no longer pink and mixture is almost cooked dry, about 7 minutes. Add cumin, salt and pepper to taste.

5. Remove from heat and fold in cheese until melted. Fold in toasted nuts, parsley and paprika.

6. Spoon equal amounts of mixture into hollowed-out caps, about 2 tsp. [10 mL] per cap, mounding the filling slightly. Arrange in a single layer in a lightly oiled baking dish.

7. Refrigerate up to 3 hours ahead of serving if you wish. To bake, preheat oven to 350°F [180°C]. Bake, uncovered, for 15 minutes or until filling is puffed and golden.

8. Let cool slightly for 5 minutes. Dust with a little paprika for colour and serve immediately.

goat cheese with green olive tapenade
MAKES 6 SERVINGS

1	[500 mL] container jumbo Greek-style pitted green olives
2	tsp. [10 mL] capers, rinsed
1	cup [250 mL] loosely packed flat-leaf Italian parsley
1/2	cup [125 mL] loosely packed cilantro
1	tsp. [5 mL] anchovy paste
1/4	cup [60 mL] olive oil, plus extra for garnish
3	[150 g] pyramid-shaped containers of goat cheese [Chèvre]

1. Place the olives, capers, parsley, cilantro and anchovy paste in the bowl of a food processor. Process until finely chopped.

2. Add the oil a little at a time and pulse until combined.

3. On a platter, arrange the three pyramids of goat cheese.

4. Spoon about 3 Tbsp. [45 mL] of olive mixture over top of each and drizzle with olive oil. Serve with unsalted crackers.

5. Leftover olive tapenade will keep for up to a month in the refrigerator. Perfect for last-minute entertaining.

Calories: 419;
Protein 17.1 g;
Carbohydrate 6.3 g;
Fibre 2.4 g;
Fat 37 g/serving

baked crab wontons

MAKES ABOUT 50 PIECES

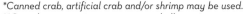

PHOTO: BRAD STRINGER

1	[250 g] pkg. cream cheese, softened
1-1/2	tsp. [8 mL] garlic purée
2	Tbsp. [30 mL] minced onion/shallot
3	small hot red/green chili peppers
1/2	tsp. [3 mL] turmeric
1/4	tsp. [1 mL] ground cumin
1/4	tsp. [1 mL] ground coriander
1/4	tsp. [1 mL] salt
	Grated peel of 2 limes
2	Tbsp. [30 mL] fresh lime juice
1	[1"/2.5 cm] piece fresh ginger, grated
3/4	lb. [375 mL] fresh crab*
	Pastry for one 9" [23 cm] double-crust pie**

*Canned crab, artificial crab and/or shrimp may be used.
**Can also use wonton wrappers or phyllo pastry.

Calories: 82;
Protein 2 g;
Carbohydrate 3 g;
Fibre 0 g;
Fat 4 g/wonton

1. Combine all ingredients except pastry in a medium bowl; mix well.

2. Preheat oven to 425°F [220°C].

3. On a floured board, roll out pastry to a large rectangle and cut into 2-1/2" [6.25 cm] squares. Place a small amount of filling in the centre of each square. Fold one corner of each square across to the opposite corner, making a triangle. Use a little water on the end of your finger to seal. Bring the two side points of the triangle up together to meet in front, leaving the third tip in place. This makes a shape somewhat like a wonton.

4. Place on ungreased cookie sheets. Bake about 20 minutes or until pastry is puffed and well browned. Cool slightly before serving.

Note: Wontons may be frozen unbaked or baked. Thaw unbaked wontons before baking as above. If reheating pre-baked wontons, place in a 350°F [180°C] oven about 10 minutes to crisp and heat. Parcels may also be made in other shapes, as long as the sides are well sealed to contain the filling.

spring vegetable terrine
MAKES 12 SERVINGS

1	large leek
1	bunch asparagus, trimmed
1	large carrot, peeled, quartered lengthwise
3	[150 g] pkgs. goat cheese [Chèvre]
1/4	tsp. [2 mL] creamed horseradish
	Salt and pepper, to taste

---

1. Bring a large pot of water to a boil. Divide the white and green parts of the leek and wash thoroughly. Blanch the leek greens in boiling water for about 2 minutes, until soft. Remove greens and rinse in cold water. Drain in a colander and set aside.

2. Steam asparagus until tender. Set aside.

3. Boil carrots until tender. Drain and set aside.

4. Meanwhile, finely slice the white parts of the leek. Over moderate heat, soften the sliced leek in a skillet with 1/4 cup [60 mL] water. Remove from heat once the water has evaporated; season with salt and pepper.

5. In a medium-size bowl, mix together the softened leek whites, goat cheese and horseradish.

6. Roll a sheet of foil into a log shape and place on one side of a loaf pan, leaving a narrower space to fill with terrine. Line the empty space with plastic wrap and allow extra to hang over all sides.

7. Separate the leek greens so that they form a single thin sheet and dry with a paper towel. Lay 1/2 the leek greens across the loaf pan mould, overlapping each one and allowing enough to overhang so that the bottom of the terrine will be enclosed.

8. Fill the bottom of the terrine with 1/3 of the goat cheese mixture. Top with 1/2 the asparagus, placing side by side in a single layer.

9. Cover asparagus with another 1/3 of cheese and then lay out the carrot pieces in three rows down the length of the mould. Cover carrot with the remaining cheese, then add another layer of asparagus.

10. Wrap the remaining leek greens over top of the asparagus and gently press to seal.

11. Finally, wrap the terrine with the overhanging plastic wrap and weight down with a plate. Place terrine in the refrigerator and chill for at least 2 hours or overnight.

12. Unwrap the terrine and gently turn it out of the mould. Run a sharp knife under hot water, before cutting the terrine into 1/2" slices.

13. Serve with thin baguette slices.

Calories: 643;
Protein 7.3 g;
Carbohydrate 73.7 g;
Fibre 1 g;
Fat 39.8 g/serving

mini turkey empanadas

MAKES ABOUT 65 PIECES

1	lb. [500 g] ground turkey or chicken
3/4	cup [175 mL] minced onion
1/4	cup [60 mL] minced green pepper
3	chipotle peppers [in adobo sauce], minced*
2	large garlic cloves, minced
2	ripe tomatoes, seeded, peeled, diced
1	Tbsp. [15 mL] minced fresh cilantro
1	tsp. [5 mL] ground cumin
1	tsp. [5 mL] crushed red pepper flakes
1/2	tsp. [3 mL] salt
1	egg beaten with a little cold water [optional]
	Pastry [homemade or frozen]**

*Available in tins in the Mexican food section.
**You will need pastry for about two 9" [23 cm] double-crust pies.

Calories: 63;
Protein 2.4 g;
Carbohydrate 5.2 g;
Fibre 0.1 g;
Fat 3.4 g/empanada

1. Preheat oven to 425°F [220°C].

2. Prepare pastry [if using homemade] and refrigerate while you make the filling.

3. For the filling, combine all ingredients except pastry and beaten egg. [Use some of the adobo sauce with the chipotle peppers.] Mix well.

4. Divide pastry into quarters and roll out each quarter to about 5/16" [8 mm] thick. Use a glass or cookie cutter [about 3"-4"/7.5-10 cm in diameter] to cut circles in the pastry. Use a small spoon to place a small amount of filling on one half of each circle. Brush circle edges with beaten egg [if using] and fold empty half over filling to make a semi-circle. Press around edges to seal.

5. Place semi-circular empanadas on ungreased baking sheets. Repeat with all pastry and all filling. Brush outsides of empanadas with beaten egg [if using]. Bake about 15-20 minutes or until pastry is golden brown. Remove to a rack to cool slightly. Serve warm with salsa and/or sour cream, if desired. Can be reheated in a warm oven [not the microwave]. Can also be frozen for warming in the oven before serving.

PHOTO: BRAD STRINGER

pink grapefruit mimosas
MAKES 4 SERVINGS

1-1/2	cups [375 mL] cold pink grapefruit juice
1	[375 mL] bottle cold sparkling wine
1/2	cup [125 mL] cold orange liqueur [or orange & brandy liqueur]
	Fresh orange segments

1. Combine juice, wine and liqueur in a pitcher; mix.
2. Pour into tall flutes, placing a couple of orange segments on cocktail picks across the top of each.

Calories: 171;
Protein 1 g;
Carbohydrate 18 g;
Fibre 0.2 g;
Fat 0 g/serving

PHOTO: ROBERT KENNEY

frosted coffee and chocolate punch

MAKES 4 SERVINGS

2	cups [500 mL] chocolate milk
1	cup [250 mL] cold, strong black coffee
6	Tbsp. [90 mL] granulated sugar
1/2	cup [125 mL] coffee liqueur
4	orange wedges
	Ice cubes

Calories: 303;
Protein 4.5 g;
Carbohydrate 53.5 g;
Fibre 0 g;
Fat 2.8 g/serving

1. Combine first 4 ingredients; mix well; refrigerate until ready to serve.

2. Fill 4 tall glasses with ice cubes.

3. Divide coffee punch among the glasses.

4. Place an orange wedge on the rim of each glass and serve at once.

pineapple tea

MAKES 4 TO 6 SERVINGS

4	cups [1 L] strong tea
1	small cheesecloth bag of whole allspice, cinnamon, cloves
1-1/2	cups [375 mL] unsweetened pineapple juice
1/4	cup [60 mL] lemon juice*
1/4	cup [60 mL] granulated sugar
	Ice cubes
	Lemon slices/pineapple spears [optional]

Fresh lemon juice works best but bottled juice can be substituted.

1. Make the tea and drop in the cheesecloth bag.
2. Remove bag when tea is cool.
3. Combine tea, juices and sugar in a pitcher; stir to mix well; refrigerate until very cold.
4. Fill 4 tall glasses with ice cubes; divide tea mixture among the 4 glasses.
5. Add a lemon slice or pineapple spear to each glass and serve.

Calories: 93;
Protein 0.3 g;
Carbohydrate 23 g;
Fibre 0.2 g;
Fat 0 g/serving

spicy virgin caesar
MAKES 1 SERVING

Ice cubes
Celery salt
Western Family Louisiana Hot Sauce
Western Family Tomato Clam Cocktail
Fresh lime juice
Lime wedge, celery stalk or marinated green bean, for garnish

---

1. Fill a tall glass with ice.
2. Add 1 shake of celery salt and 3-5 drops Hot Sauce.
3. Fill glass with Tomato Clam Cocktail.
4. Add about 1/2 tsp. [2 mL] fresh lime juice. Stir well.
5. Garnish with a celery stalk or a marinated green bean and a lime wedge.

Serving suggestions: Try making decorative ice cubes to add colour, flavour and interest to your favourite drinks.
• For iced teas or lemonade, freeze prepared tea or lemonade in ice-cube trays. Store in a plastic bag until needed.
• For fizzy, fruity drinks, freeze ginger ale or club soda in ice-cube trays.
• For added colour, fill ice-cube trays halfway with water. When almost set, press a berry, edible flower or a lemon twist into each ice cube. Cover with water and continue freezing until set.

Calories: 60;
Protein 1 g;
Carbohydrate 11 g;
Fibre 2.5 g;
Fat 0 g/serving

PHOTO: PHILIPPE MARTIN-MORICE

watermelon berry virgin margarita

MAKES 4 SERVINGS

2	cups [500 mL] frozen watermelon cubes*
1	cup [250 mL] fresh watermelon cubes
1	cup [250 mL] raspberry sorbet
1	Tbsp. [15 mL] fresh lime juice
1/2	cup [125 mL] ice cubes
	Cold water
	Lime juice and granulated sugar, for garnish

*Freeze fresh cubes of watermelon for about 4 hours.

1. Combine first 5 ingredients together in a blender and process to desired consistency.
2. Add cold water as needed.
3. Serve in a sugar-rimmed glass, made by dipping the rim of each glass in lime juice, then granulated sugar.

Calories: 129;
Protein 1.75 g;
Carbohydrate 29 g;
Fibre 2.3 g;
Fat 1.75 g/serving

PHOTO: ROBERT KENNEY

winter marsala chai

MAKES 6 SERVINGS

1	bag English Breakfast tea
1	Tbsp. [15 mL] whole cardamom
2	large cinnamon sticks
1/2	tsp. [3 mL] whole cloves
2	whole star anise
1/4	tsp. [2 mL] ground ginger

Calories: 20;
Protein 0.6 g;
Carbohydrate 4.9 g;
Fibre 0 g;
Fat 0.5 g/serving
with milk

1. Fill a medium teapot with boiling water.

2. Add tea bag and spices; let steep, covered, for approximately 5 minutes.

3. Remove tea bag only and let tea steep another 10 minutes.

4. Strain spices through a tea strainer into tea cups.

5. Serve with cream or milk and sugar.

apple blackcurrant cider
MAKES 6 SERVINGS

4	cups [1 L] unsweetened apple cider
2	Tbsp. [30 mL] blackcurrant syrup*
1	tsp. [5 mL] whole cloves
1	tsp. [5 mL] whole allspice
2	large cinnamon sticks
1	Tbsp. [15 mL] brown sugar, or to taste
1	Tbsp. [15 mL] grated orange peel

*We used Ribena Concentrate.

1. In a saucepan, combine all ingredients; simmer over medium heat for 10-15 minutes.
2. Strain hot cider and serve in mugs with cinnamon sticks and orange peel for garnish.

Note: The longer the cider simmers, the stronger the flavour of the spices.

The scent of cinnamon: Cinnamon is the aromatic inner bark of an evergreen tree in the laurel family native to Sri Lanka, India and Burma. This spice, once considered more valuable than gold, is used to flavour everything from curries to sweet rolls. While it's best known for its role in cooking and as a swizzle stick for hot beverages, cinnamon can also be used to delicately scent the air. Wrap a cinnamon stick, a dozen cloves and the peel of one orange in a piece of cheesecloth, then drop the package into a small pot of boiling water. The simmering heat releases the essential oils in the ingredients allowing them to envelope your home in warm, citrus-spice fragrance. The evaporating water has a humidifying effect, too, which will be welcome on a cold winter day.

Calories: 96;
Protein 0.3 g;
Carbohydrate 24 g;
Fibre 0 g;
Fat 0.4 g/serving

[soups & salads]

Chicken Gumbo

Perfectly Simple Onion Soup

Mushroom Soup with Caramelized Onions

Roasted Corn and Crab Chowder

Spring Pea Soup

Smoky Black Bean Soup

Bean and Lentil Tomato Chowder

Roasted Butternut Squash Soup with Garlic Cream

Potato and Cabbage Soup

Simple Seafood Chowder

Sumptuous Asian Soup

Roasted Harvest Vegetable Soup

Thai Pasta Salad

Salmon Salad Niçoise

Spanish Rice Salad

Spinach Salad

Hot Potato Salad

Marinated Bean and Mushroom Salad

Tomato Bocconcini Salad

Fresh Crab and Mango Salad

Beet and Pear Salad

Cold Asparagus Salad

Spinach and Apple Salad with Poppy Seed Dressing

Wild Greens with Raspberry Dressing

Tabbouleh Salad

Layered Vegetable Salad

chicken gumbo

MAKES 8 SERVINGS

4	slices lean bacon
6	Tbsp. [90 mL] flour
1	cup [250 mL] diced onion
1/2	cup [125 mL] diced green bell pepper
1/2	cup [125 mL] diced celery
2	red or green Jalapeños, seeded, minced
1	[28 fl. oz./796 mL] tin chicken broth*
2	[10 fl. oz./284 mL] tins chicken broth*
3	cups [750 mL] diced cooked chicken [or turkey]
1/2	tsp. [3 mL] coarse black pepper
1/2	tsp. [3 mL] cajun seasoning**
1	cup [250 mL] long grain white rice
1/4	cup [60 mL] chopped parsley
	vegetable oil

*Use low-fat chicken broth, if you can find it.
**We used Hy's Louisiana Black Cajun Seasoning, but any Cajun seasoning powder will do.

Calories: 305;
Protein 18 g;
Carbohydrate 29 g;
Fibre 1.5 g;
Fat 13 g/serving

1. Dice bacon and cook in a large Dutch oven over medium heat until crisp. Remove; set aside.
2. Measure fat left in pan. Make up to 4 Tbsp. [60 mL] with vegetable oil, if needed. Heat the fat until very hot; stir in flour. Stir and cook until roux [fat and flour mixture] turns medium-brown in colour. [This should take up to 15 minutes.]
3. Add diced onion, green bell pepper and celery; stir in to coat well with roux.
4. Add Jalapeños, chicken broth, chicken, seasonings and rice; stir; cover and cook until rice is tender [about 20 minutes].
5. Add parsley and heat 1 minute.
6. Serve at once in heated bowls. Sprinkle with reserved cooked bacon bits.

perfectly simple onion soup with baked cheese crostinis

MAKES 6 SERVINGS

2	Tbsp. [30 mL] olive oil
2-1/2	lbs. [1.25 kg] yellow onions
1	Tbsp. [15 mL] maple syrup
4	cups [1 L] beef broth
2	tsp. [10 mL] Dijon mustard
2	tsp. [10 mL] good-quality Balsamic vinegar
1/4	tsp. [1 mL] each salt and freshly ground black pepper
6	slices sourdough baguette, cut on a diagonal
1/3	cup [75 mL] grated Emmenthal or Swiss cheese
2	Tbsp. [30 mL] crumbled Stilton or blue cheese
	cooking spray

1. Heat oil in a large, heavy-bottomed saucepan.

2. Peel and slice onions and separate into rings. They should measure about 3 quarts [3 L]. Stir into oil in pan along with maple syrup and cover.

3. Cook over medium heat for 20 minutes, stirring occasionally. Onions will begin to sweat and soften. Remove lid and continue to cook for another 10 minutes, stirring often until onions begin to cook dry and turn golden.

4. Stir in broth, mustard, Balsamic and seasonings; bring to a boil. Reduce heat. Angle lid to allow steam to escape; simmer for another 10 minutes.

5. Preheat oven to 350°F [180°C].

6. To make crostinis, lightly spray baguette slices on both sides with cooking spray. Spread out on a baking sheet and bake for 2 minutes. Remove from the oven.

7. Using tongs, flip slices. Top each with grated Emmenthal and crumbled Stilton.

8. Return to oven and bake for 1 more minute or until cheeses melt.

9. Ladle soup into bowls and float a crostini on each.

10. Serve immediately. Cheese will be very hot. Soup is excellent if made a day or two ahead and refrigerated before reheating and serving.

Calories: 272;
Protein 11 g;
Carbohydrate 33.8 g;
Fibre 4.1 g;
Fat 10.8 g/serving

mushroom soup with caramelized onions

MAKES 8 CUPS [2 L]

3	Tbsp. [45 mL] olive oil, divided
2	medium onions, sliced, about 3 cups [750 mL]
4	large garlic cloves, minced
2	medium potatoes, peeled, finely diced, about 1-1/2 cups [375 mL]
1	lb. [500 g] button mushrooms, thickly sliced [about 4 c./1 L]
1/2	cup [125 mL] medium dry sherry
1	lb. [500 g] mushrooms such as Shiitake, oyster and crimini, thickly sliced [about 4 c./1 L]
2	cups [500 mL] vegetable or beef broth
2	cups [500 mL] water
1	Tbsp. [15 mL] soy sauce
1	tsp. [5 mL] dried marjoram
1	tsp. [5 mL] dried leaf thyme
1/4	cup [60 mL] whipping cream [optional]
	Freshly squeezed lemon juice [optional]
	Generous pinches of sea salt and freshly ground black pepper

*Calories: 165;
Protein 5.1 g;
Carbohydrate 17.5 g;
Fibre 3.1 g;
Fat 8.4 g/1 cup
[250 mL] serving*

1. Heat 1 Tbsp. [15 mL] oil in a large heavy saucepan.

2. Break onions into rings and add. Sprinkle with salt and pepper. Sauté over medium heat about 15 minutes or until onions start to soften. Stir often to prevent sticking.

3. Add minced garlic and diced potatoes and continue to cook another 10 minutes or until onions and potatoes begin to turn golden. Stir often.

4. Deglaze pan with sherry. Boil vigorously until reduced by half and potatoes are tender.

5. Purée onions and potatoes using a handheld blender, or purée in two batches in a blender or food processor until smooth. Return to saucepan.

6. While onions are cooking, heat 1 Tbsp. oil [15 mL] in a separate heavy pot. Add half the mushrooms and a generous sprinkling of salt and pepper and sauté over medium-high heat. As the mushrooms cook they will release some of their juices and begin to stick to the pan. Continue to sear mushrooms over medium-high heat without stirring, until golden, about 7 or 8 minutes.

7. Using a spatula, flip mushrooms and continue to sear a couple minutes longer, until golden and almost tender. Remove to a bowl.

8. Heat remaining 1 Tbsp. [15 mL] oil in heavy saucepan and add remaining mushrooms and repeat cooking and searing until golden and almost tender.

9. Add all seared mushrooms to puréed onions along with broth, water, soy sauce and seasonings. Stir together, scraping the bottom of the pan, and bring to a boil.

11. Cover, reduce heat and cook over medium-low heat 20-30 minutes to allow flavours to blend. Serve as is or with a little fresh lemon juice squeezed over each serving.

roasted corn and crab chowder

MAKES 6 SERVINGS

4	cobs corn [in husks] or 2 cups [500 mL] cooked corn
6	slices lean bacon, chopped*
2	Tbsp. [30 mL] unsalted butter**
4	garlic cloves, minced
1	large onion, diced
2	[14 fl. oz./398 mL] tins clam nectar
1	cup [250 mL] instant mashed potato flakes
1/2	cup [125 mL] light cream
4	tsp. [20 mL] chopped fresh thyme
1	tsp. [5 mL] Cajun Blackened Seasoning mix
1/2	tsp. [3 mL] salt
1/2	lb. [250 g] fresh crab meat

*You can also use half a jar of Real Bacon Pieces or Bits if you prefer; eliminate the bacon cooking and add at the end of the recipe.
**If using the jar of Real Bacon, increase butter to 1/4 cup [60 mL]. Unsalted butter is best in Cajun or Creole dishes.

1. Place corn under broiler or on barbecue until husks are blackened on all sides. Cool; cut off kernels [you should have about 2 c./500 mL].
2. Heat Dutch oven; add bacon and cook until crisp; remove with slotted spoon.
3. Add butter to pan; when sizzling, add garlic and onion. When onion is nearly tender, add nectar and potato flakes.
4. Cook, stirring occasionally until thickened slightly. Reduce heat to simmer; add corn kernels, cream, thyme, seasoning mix, salt and bacon. Simmer 20 minutes.
5. Add crab; heat 5-10 minutes.
6. Serve in heated bowls, topped with a sprinkling of the Cajun Blackened Seasoning mix.

Calories: 363;
Protein 15 g;
Carbohydrate 24 g;
Fibre 4 g;
Fat 23 g/serving

spring pea soup with gremolata and extra virgin olive oil splash

MAKES 4 ENTRÉE OR 6 APPETIZER SERVINGS

4	Tbsp. [60 mL] garlic butter*
2	cooking onions, diced
2	large baking potatoes, peeled, diced
2	lbs. [1 kg] fresh shelled or frozen peas
6	[10 fl. oz./284 mL] tins vegetable broth with onions
4	tsp. [20 mL] McCormick's No Salt Citrus & Pepper Seasoning**
1	tsp. [5 mL] coarse black pepper
2/3	cup [150 mL] no-fat sour cream

Gremolata:

6	Tbsp. [90 mL] shredded sugar snap peas
	Grated peel of 2 lemons
4	tsp. [20 mL] McCormick's No Salt Citrus & Pepper Seasoning**
	Extra virgin olive oil [optional]

Available in 1/4 lb. [125 g] sticks in the dairy section.
**Or substitute any similar garlic and herb seasoning.*

Calories: 515;
Protein 25 g;
Carbohydrate 68 g;
Fibre 15 g;
Fat 17 g/entrée serving

1. Heat the garlic butter in a Dutch oven until bubbly. Add onion and potato and cook until onion is softened.

2. Add peas, broth, and seasonings. Partially cover and cook over medium heat about 15 minutes or until peas are tender.

3. Purée the soup in a food processor until smooth. Push through a fine sieve and place in a saucepan back on the heat. Keep heat at low and stir in sour cream. Heat gently 1-2 minutes.

4. Meanwhile, combine gremolata ingredients except olive oil. Serve soup in heated bowls with the gremolata sprinkled over top of each bowl. Offer extra virgin olive oil for sprinkling over soup, if desired.

spring pea
soup with
gremolata

PHOTO: JOHN SINAL

smoky black
bean soup

smoky black bean soup

MAKES 8 CUPS [2 L]

2	Tbsp. [30 mL] vegetable oil
1	large onion, diced
8	garlic cloves, minced
2	tsp. [10 mL] coriander seeds
2	tsp. [10 mL] cumin seeds
1	tsp. [5 mL] dried oregano leaves
2/3	cup [150 mL] fresh orange juice
2	[19 fl. oz./540 mL] tins black beans, drained, rinsed, divided
1	[28 fl. oz./796 mL] tin plum tomatoes, including juice
2	cups [500 mL] vegetable broth or bouillon
1-2	chipotle peppers [in adobo sauce], minced*
1	bay leaf
1/2	each red, yellow and green bell pepper, diced
	Juice of 1 lime
	Crème fraîche or light sour cream [optional]

*Available in tins in the Mexican foods section.

1. Heat oil in a large heavy saucepan. Add onion and garlic and sauté over medium-low heat until onion is soft, about 7 minutes. Be careful not to brown or scorch. Stir often.

2. While onion is sautéing, place coriander and cumin seeds in a small dry pan over low heat. Stir and shake seeds for about a minute until they begin to release an aroma. Sprinkle with oregano leaves and continue to shake over low heat another minute or just until they begin to darken slightly.

3. Transfer to the bowl of a mortar and pestle or a spice grinder and crush to a coarse powder. Sprinkle over sautéed onions and stir in.

4. Add orange juice and deglaze pan. Cook over medium heat until juice is reduced by half. Reserve 1 cup [250 mL] black beans and set aside. Stir in remaining beans.

5. Add tomatoes and their juice, vegetable broth, chipotle peppers and bay leaf. Break up tomatoes with a fork. Bring soup to a boil. Cover, reduce heat and simmer for 30 minutes to allow flavours to blend.

6. Stir in reserved black beans, diced peppers and lime juice and heat through. Serve with crème fraîche or sour cream, if you wish.

Calories: 272; Protein 14.8 g; Carbohydrate 44.8 g; Fibre 10 g; Fat 4.8 g/1 cup [250 mL] serving

bean and lentil tomato chowder

MAKES 4 ENTREE SERVINGS

1	Tbsp. [15 mL] olive oil
1	medium onion, diced
3	garlic cloves, minced
2	large carrots, diced
1/2	cup [125 mL] red and/or green lentils, soaked 1 hour
1	[28 fl. oz./796 mL] tin diced tomatoes, including juice
2	Tbsp. [30 mL] tomato paste
2	[10 fl. oz./284 mL] tins chicken broth
1	[10 fl. oz./284 mL] tin beef broth
3/4	tsp. [4 mL] coarse black pepper
1/2	tsp. [3 mL] salt
3	Tbsp. [45 mL] minced fresh oregano
1	[14 fl. oz./398 mL] tin red kidney beans, rinsed
1	[14 fl. oz./398 mL] tin pinto beans, rinsed
1	Tbsp. [15 mL] Worcestershire sauce
1	Tbsp. [15 mL] Balsamic vinegar

Calories: 427;
Protein 27 g;
Carbohydrate 64 g;
Fibre 17 g;
Fat 7 g/serving;

1. Heat oil in a large soup pot. When hot, add onion, garlic and carrot.
2. Sauté until carrot is just tender, stirring frequently. Add drained lentils; stir to coat lentils and cook 5 minutes.
3. Add tomatoes, tomato paste, broths, pepper, salt and oregano. Tilt lid and cook at a strong simmer for about 1-3/4 to 2 hours, or until lentils are nearly tender.
4. Add both beans and Worcestershire. Heat another 15 minutes.
5. Add Balsamic vinegar and heat another 15 minutes.
6. Serve at once in heated soup bowls.

roasted butternut squash soup with garlic cream

MAKES 8 SERVINGS

4	lb. [2 kg] butternut squash [approx. 2 to 3 small], halved lengthwise
2	whole heads garlic
3	Tbsp. [45 mL] olive oil
2	medium red onions, about 3 cups [750 mL], coarsely chopped
5	garlic cloves, peeled, chopped
1	tsp. [5 mL] Madras curry powder
5	cups [1.25 L] vegetable stock
3/4	cup [175 mL] low-fat buttermilk
1/2	cup [125 mL] low-fat yogurt
1/4	cup [60 mL] pecans, toasted, coarsely chopped
	Salt and freshly ground pepper

1. Preheat oven to 375°F [190°C].
2. Line a large baking sheet with aluminum foil and lightly oil. Place squash, cut-side down on the foil.
3. Slice 1/3 off the root end of the garlic heads; place in a square of aluminum foil. Drizzle with a little olive oil and twist the foil around the heads to enclose them completely. Place the garlic package onto the baking sheet. Bake the squash and garlic for 45 to 55 minutes or until squash is very tender when pierced with a fork and the garlic is soft and caramel coloured; cool slightly.
4. In a large heavy saucepan, heat 3 Tbsp. [45 mL] oil over medium heat. Add onions and sauté until softened and translucent. Add the 5 garlic cloves, curry powder, and salt and pepper to taste. Cook, stirring until fragrant, about 3 minutes.
5. Scrape the seeds from the squash and discard. Remove the flesh from squash shells, scraping with a spoon; discard the outer skin.
6. Add squash to the casserole, along with vegetable stock. Bring to a boil; reduce heat to medium-low and simmer for 40-45 minutes. The squash should be soft and falling apart.
7. Purée soup in batches using a handheld blender or food processor; return to the cleaned casserole. Stir in buttermilk; keep warm.
8. While soup is cooking, remove garlic heads from foil and squeeze cloves into the bowl of a food processor. Add yogurt and purée until smooth. Transfer to a small bowl.
9. Ladle the soup into warmed soup bowls and garnish with a swirl of the garlic yogurt mixture and a sprinkle of toasted pecans. Thin, if necessary, with a little water or buttermilk.

Calories: 235; Protein 6.1 g; Carbohydrate 40 g; Fibre 6.5 g; Fat 8.2 g/serving

PHOTO: JOHN SHERLOCK

potato and cabbage soup

MAKES 4 TO 6 ENTRÉE SERVINGS

6	slices lean bacon, diced
2	onions, thinly sliced*
3	celery stalks, thinly sliced*
2	large carrots, thinly sliced*
3/4	cup [175 mL] all-purpose flour
1	tsp. [5 mL] granulated sugar
2	Tbsp. [30 mL] Balsamic vinegar
3	baking potatoes, peeled, chopped
1	qt. [1 L] chicken broth
2	cups [500 mL] shredded Savoy or other green cabbage
1	cup [250 mL] 1% buttermilk
2-3	Tbsp. [30-45 mL] chopped fresh dill
	Salt and coarse black pepper, to taste

Slicing the vegetables on a mandolin makes the slices thinner – and it's easier!

*Calories: 226;
Protein 11 g;
Carbohydrate 41 g;
Fibre 6 g;
Fat 2.2 g/serving*

1. Add the bacon to a hot Dutch oven. Cook until crisp; remove with a slotted spoon, leaving the fat in the pan.
2. While the bacon is cooking, combine the onion, celery and carrot slices in a plastic or paper bag. Toss with enough flour to coat [may be more or less than the suggested amount]. Remove from bag, leaving excess flour behind.
3. Add to hot bacon fat. Reduce heat to low, cover and cook 15 minutes, stirring occasionally.
4. Add sugar and Balsamic vinegar to vegetables and cook another 10 minutes with the lid on.
5. Add potato cubes and chicken broth; stir and cook over medium heat about 30 minutes or until potato cubes are just tender.
6. Add bacon and cabbage to pan; stir and cook another 15 minutes.
7. Stir in buttermilk and dill. Cook another 5 minutes; add salt and pepper to taste.
8. Serve at once with a dollop of sour cream on top if desired.

simple seafood chowder

MAKES 6 ENTREE SERVINGS

4	slices lean bacon, chopped
1	cup [250 mL] chopped onion
3	garlic cloves, minced
1	small green bell pepper, seeded, diced
3	[14 fl. oz./398 mL] tins clam nectar
1-1/2	cups [375 mL] instant mashed potato flakes
	Grated peel and juice of 1 small lemon
1/4	tsp. [2 mL] cayenne
3-4	Tbsp. [45-60 mL] minced fresh herbs [thyme, rosemary, sage, etc.]
1/4	tsp. [2 mL] salt
1/4	tsp. [2 mL] coarse black pepper
1	lb. [500 g] cod/snapper/salmon fillets [or mixed]
1	[142 g] tin clams, undrained
1/4	lb. [125 g] machine-peeled fresh shrimp
1/2	cup [125 mL] original or regular soy beverage

1. Cook bacon in a large soup pot until crisp. Remove with a slotted spoon.

2. In remaining fat, cook onion, garlic and pepper until just tender.

3. Add clam nectar and mashed potato flakes; tilt lid. Simmer 10 minutes, stirring occasionally.

4. Add lemon peel and juice, cayenne, herbs, salt and pepper, crisp bacon, and the fish fillets, cut into bite-sized chunks. Tilt lid again and cook another 5 minutes.

5. Add clams, shrimp and soy beverage. Tilt lid and cook another 5 minutes.

6. Serve at once in heated soup bowls.

Calories: 288;
Protein 28 g;
Carbohydrate 17 g;
Fibre 2 g;
Fat 12 g/serving

sumptuous asian soup

MAKES 4 SERVINGS

2	[10 fl. oz./284 mL] tins chicken broth
1	[500 g] bag frozen Japanese-style vegetables
1	cup [250 mL] vermicelli or fine egg noodles
1/2	[300 g] pkg. firm tofu, cut into 1" x 1/4" [2.5 x 0.6 cm] cubes
1	tsp. [5 mL] sesame oil
3/4	tsp. [4 mL] hot sauce
2	Tbsp. [30 mL] cornstarch
3	whole green onions, diagonally sliced
	Freshly ground black pepper

Calories: 292;
Protein 23 g;
Carbohydrate 32 g;
Fibre 5.3 g;
Fat 10 g/serving

1. Heat broth plus 2 tins water in a large saucepan until boiling.

2. Add frozen vegetables and return to a boil. Reduce heat to medium and add vermicelli noodles and tofu. Cook for 3-5 minutes or until vermicelli is plumped and tofu hot.

3. Add sesame oil and hot sauce.

4. Dissolve cornstarch in 1/4 cup [60 mL] cold water. Stir into broth and continue to cook, stirring frequently until soup is slightly glazed, about 3 more minutes.

5. Sprinkle with green onions and freshly ground black pepper. Soup is also excellent with fresh prawns or chicken strips stirred into broth.

roasted harvest vegetable soup

MAKES 10 CUPS [2.5 L]

2	acorn or butternut squash, about 4 lbs. [2 kg]
4	tomatoes
8	large garlic cloves, peeled
1	large cooking onion, peeled, cut into wedges
2	large carrots, peeled, coarsely chopped
2	medium potatoes, peeled, chopped
1-1/2	Tbsp. [25 mL] olive oil
1/2	tsp. [3 mL] salt
8-9	cups [2-2.25 L] vegetable stock, heated
1/4	tsp. [2 mL] saffron, crushed

1. Preheat oven to 375°F [190°C].
2. Cut squash in half lengthwise and scrape out the seeds. Place cut side down on a lightly oiled baking sheet. Bake in the lower part of the preheated oven until tender when pierced with a fork, about 30 minutes.
3. Core tomatoes and cut in half. Combine in a bowl with peeled garlic cloves, onion wedges, carrots and potatoes. Drizzle with oil and salt. Toss together.
4. Transfer to a parchment-lined roasting pan spreading into a single layer. Be sure to place tomato halves cut side down. Roast in the upper portion of the oven for about 30 minutes or until vegetables begin to darken and garlic is golden.
5. When vegetables have finished roasting, transfer to a large heavy-bottomed saucepan along with any juices that may have accumulated in the roasting pan.
6. When squash is cool enough to handle, scoop flesh from the rinds and add to saucepan. Stir in enough heated broth to cover vegetables. Stir in saffron and bring to a boil. Reduce heat to simmer. Cover, leaving lid ajar, and simmer for 20 minutes to blend the flavours.
7. Remove from the heat and purée soup in batches until smooth. Refrigerate overnight or freeze if not serving right away.
8. To serve, gently reheat soup, whisking occasionally until hot. Ladle into soup bowls and serve.

Calories 157;
Protein 4 g;
Carbohydrate 31.1 g;
Fibre 6.3 g;
Fat 3.5 g/1 cup
[250 mL] serving

thai pasta salad

MAKES 4 SERVINGS

1	small, whole bone-in chicken breast, about 3/4 lb. [375 g], skinned, trimmed
2	tsp. [10 mL] vegetable oil
2	Tbsp. [30 mL] finely chopped fresh ginger
2	Tbsp. [30 mL] finely chopped garlic
2	Tbsp. [30 mL] finely chopped shallot
1/2	cup [125 mL] crunchy natural peanut butter
3	Tbsp. [45 mL] soy sauce
3	Tbsp. [45 mL] freshly squeezed lime juice
1	Tbsp. [15 mL] sesame oil
2	Tbsp. [30 mL] rice wine vinegar
1	Tbsp. [15 mL] packed brown sugar
1/2	tsp. [3 mL] crushed red pepper flakes
1/3	cup [75 mL] finely chopped cilantro
1/3	cup [75 mL] finely chopped mint
1/2	cup [125 mL] finely sliced green onion
1/2	cup [125 mL] peeled, coarsely shredded carrot
1/4	cup [60 mL] coarsely chopped roasted peanuts
1/2	lb. [225 g] dry spaghettini pasta, cooked al dente

Calories: 580;
Protein 39 g;
Carbohydrate 61 g;
Fibre 5.1 g;
Fat 20 g/serving

1. Place chicken breast in a large saucepan; fill it with enough cold water to cover completely. Season lightly with salt and pepper; bring water to a boil; then reduce heat to medium low. The water should be at a gentle simmer. Poach for 25 minutes.
2. Allow chicken to cool in the cooking liquid. Remove chicken from the pan, reserving the cooking liquid. Pull the chicken meat from the bone; cut it into 1/2" [1.25 cm] pieces. Chill until ready to use.
3. In a small saucepan, over medium heat, heat the vegetable oil. Add ginger, garlic and shallot; cook 4-5 minutes.
4. Transfer to a large bowl; add the peanut butter, soy sauce, lime juice, sesame oil, vinegar, brown sugar, pepper flakes and 1/2 cup [125 mL] reserved cooking liquid. Stir with a wooden spoon until the sauce is smooth; add all the remaining ingredients, including chicken.
5. Toss the pasta salad gently but thoroughly. Season with salt and freshly ground pepper. If the sauce is too thick, add a little more reserved cooking liquid. The sauce should just lightly coat the pasta.
6. Store the salad, well covered, in the refrigerator. Pack the salad into portable containers with tight-fitting lids.

Note: Add 1/2 cup [125 mL] leftover steamed vegetables to this salad, if desired.

salmon salad niçoise

MAKES 6 SERVINGS

Mustard Vinaigrette:
- 2 Tbsp. [30 mL] finely chopped shallot
- 2 Tbsp. [30 mL] Dijon mustard
- 4 Tbsp. [60 mL] sherry or red wine vinegar
- 3 Tbsp. [45 mL] finely chopped fresh parsley
- 12 Tbsp. [180 mL] olive oil
- Salt and freshly ground black pepper to taste

Salad:
- 6 small red-skinned potatoes, scrubbed
- 1/2 lb. [250 g] tender green beans, trimmed
- 3 eggs, hard-cooked
- 1 small red onion, peeled, thinly sliced
- 1 lb. [500 g] salmon fillet, cooked,chilled
- 6 cups [1.5 L] mixed young salad greens, washed and dried
- 1 cup [250 mL] assorted cherry tomatoes, stemmed
- 1/2 cup [125 mL] oil-cured black and green olives
- 2 Tbsp. [30 mL] capers
- 6 anchovies for garnish [optional]
- Fresh basil sprigs, for garnish

1. To make the vinaigrette, combine all dressing ingredients in a small bowl. Whisk thoroughly to combine. Set aside until ready to use.

2. Place potatoes in a saucepan and cover completely with cold water. Bring the water to a boil and cook until tender, about 18 minutes. Remove the potatoes with a slotted spoon and allow to cool before slicing into quarters; set aside.

3. Meanwhile, bring the saucepan of water back to the boil, add the green beans and cook until tender but still crisp, 3-5 minutes. Drain the beans, refresh under cold running water; set aside.

4. Peel the eggs, cut into quarters and set aside. Thoroughly rinse the onion rings under cold running water; set aside. Peel off large chunks of the salmon using a fork, discarding all skin and bones; set aside.

5. When ready to serve, toss the salad greens with 3 Tbsp. [45 mL] of the vinaigrette. Divide the salad between 6 chilled salad plates.

6. Arrange the potatoes, beans, eggs, onion, salmon, cherry tomatoes, olives and capers on top of the greens. Drizzle the vinaigrette over the salads, reserving any extra for passing at the table. Garnish with the anchovies and fresh basil sprigs.

7. Serve immediately with crusty multi-grain baguettes.

Calories: 514; Protein 30 g; Carbohydrate 40 g; Fibre 5.1 g; Fat 27 g/serving

spanish rice salad

MAKES 8 TO 10 SERVINGS

Rice:

1	Tbsp. [15 mL]	olive oil
2	cups [500 mL]	long grain white rice
1	tsp. [5 mL]	Spanish saffron
3-1/2	cups [875 mL]	water
1/2	tsp. [3 mL]	salt

Vinaigrette:

1/3	cup [75 mL]	freshly squeezed lime juice
3	Tbsp. [45 mL]	freshly squeezed orange juice
3	Tbsp. [45 mL]	red wine vinegar
2	tsp. [10 mL]	cumin powder
1	tsp. [5 mL]	finely chopped garlic
1/3	cup [75 mL]	extra virgin olive oil

Salad:

1	cup [250 mL]	diced roasted red bell pepper
1	cup [250 mL]	Kalamata olives
3		chorizo sausages, cooked, halved lengthwise and sliced into 1/4" [0.6 cm] thick slices
1/2	cup [125 mL]	finely chopped parsley
6		finely chopped cilantro sprigs
6		cherry tomatoes, quartered
		Salt and freshly ground black pepper, to taste

Calories: 353;
Protein 7 g;
Carbohydrate 38 g;
Fibre 2 g;
Fat 19.5 g/serving

1. In a large saucepan over low heat, combine olive oil, rice and saffron. Stir well, making sure that all the rice grains are coated with oil. Add water and salt; bring to a boil; stir gently; cover saucepan with a tight-fitting lid. Immediately reduce the heat to low; cook rice for 18 minutes; spoon the hot rice into a large bowl, fluff lightly with a fork and allow to cool.

2. Meanwhile, prepare the vinaigrette: In a small jar with a tight-fitting lid combine all of the vinaigrette ingredients. Cover tightly with the lid; shake well to combine.

3. When the rice has cooled, pour vinaigrette over the rice; add the roasted red peppers, whole olives, chorizo, parsley, cilantro and cherry tomatoes. Stir gently but thoroughly to combine, coating evenly with the vinaigrette.

4. Season to taste with salt and freshly ground black pepper. Store in the refrigerator, tightly covered, until serving time.

spinach salad

MAKES 4 SERVINGS

12	slices lean bacon
2	red bell peppers
6	eggs, hard-cooked
18	button mushrooms, sliced
2	bunches spinach
4	garlic cloves, minced
2	Tbsp. [30 mL] red wine vinegar
1	tsp. [5 mL] granulated sugar
1	tsp. [5 mL] dry English mustard
1	tsp. [5 mL] salt
1/2	tsp. [3 mL] coarse black pepper
1/4	cup [60 mL] mayonnaise
3/4	cup [175 mL] no-fat sour cream
	Chopped fresh parsley

1. Preheat broiler. Cook bacon [broiler, microwave or skillet] until crisp; drain well; chop.
2. Halve peppers and remove seeds and membranes; place on a baking sheet under broiler; broil until very black; place in a small paper bag for about half an hour; pull off blackened skin; cut into julienne strips and set aside.
3. Peel and slice eggs.
4. Combine bacon, pepper strips, egg slices and sliced mushrooms in a very large bowl.
5. Wash and thoroughly dry spinach leaves [stems removed]; tear bigger leaves into bite-size pieces; add to bowl; place in refrigerator while you prepare the dressing.
6. Combine garlic, vinegar, sugar, mustard, salt, pepper, mayonnaise and sour cream in a small bowl; beat or whisk until well combined.
7. Toss dressing with salad ingredients until all pieces are thoroughly coated. Use the amount of dressing you prefer.

Serving suggestion: Pile salad onto 4 cold plates; sprinkle with chopped parsley and serve at once with fresh focaccia.

Calories: 380;
Protein 22 g;
Carbohydrate 19 g;
Fibre 4.8 g;
Fat 24 g/serving

hot potato salad

MAKES 4 TO 6 SERVINGS

2-1/2	lbs. [1.25 kg]	potatoes, peeled, cubed, cooked
1/2	cup [125 mL]	light Italian dressing
3/4	Tbsp. [12 mL]	Dijon mustard
1/4	tsp. [1 mL]	salt
3/4	tsp. [4 mL]	creamy horseradish
1/2	tsp. [3 mL]	crushed red pepper flakes
1/4	cup [60 mL]	light mayonnaise
1/4		large red onion, cut into tiny dice
1/2		small unpeeled English cucumber, diced

Calories: 259;
Protein 4 g;
Carbohydrate 45 g;
Fibre 4.6 g;
Fat 7 g/serving

1. Place hot cooked potatoes in a large bowl.
2. Combine all other ingredients; mix well.
3. Add mixture to potatoes in bowl; toss to coat all ingredients.
4. Serve at once or store covered in the refrigerator and reheat the next day.

hot
potato
salad

marinated
bean and
mushroom
salad

marinated bean and mushroom salad

MAKES 6 SERVINGS

1	lb. [500 g] fresh green beans, trimmed, cut in 2 or 3 pieces
24	red or yellow cherry tomatoes, halved
1/2	lb. [250 g] button mushrooms, halved or quartered
1	large red onion, chunked
1	[200 g] pkg. firm tofu, diced
1/4	cup [60 mL] chopped fresh cilantro

Dressing:

2	tsp. [10 mL] minced garlic
3	Tbsp. [45 mL] malt vinegar
1/2	tsp. [3 mL] salt
3/4	tsp. [4 mL] coarse black pepper
1	tsp. [5 mL] turmeric
1/8	tsp. [1 mL] cayenne
1	tsp. [5 mL] ground coriander
1	Tbsp. [15 mL] garam masala
6	Tbsp. [90 mL] extra virgin olive oil

1. Trim and cut the beans and either microwave or boil in salted water for 6-7 minutes until partially cooked but still slightly crispy. Rinse in cold water and drain well.

2. Combine cold beans with tomatoes, mushrooms, red onion and tofu. Mix well.

3. Combine all the dressing ingredients in a bowl with a handheld blender or in a food processor. Process until well combined and slightly thickened.

4. Pour over the salad in a non-metallic bowl or casserole and mix well. Cover and refrigerate overnight or at least 6 hours.

5. Mix well before serving and sprinkle chopped cilantro over top. This salad is perfect for picnics as it can be transported with ease in a covered plastic bowl. Mix again at your destination.

Calories: 128;
Protein 8.5 g;
Carbohydrate 14.8 g;
Fibre 2.6 g;
Fat 5.6 g/serving

PHOTO: JOHN SINAL

tomato bocconcini salad

MAKES 4 SERVINGS

1	cup [250 mL] packed fresh basil leaves
2	Tbsp. [30 mL] chopped walnuts
1/2	tsp. [3 mL] salt
2	large garlic cloves, coarsely chopped
3/4	tsp. [4 mL] coarse black pepper
3	Tbsp. [45 mL] extra virgin olive oil, divided
3	Tbsp. [45 mL] Balsamic vinegar, divided
2	large ripe tomatoes*
1	tub [6 balls] fresh Bocconcini [fresh Mozzarella cheese] cut into slices
	Mixed baby mesclun greens**

*For added colour, experiment with different kinds of your favourite seasonal tomatoes.
**We used commercially packaged "Spring" mix.

Calories: 268;
Protein 10 g;
Carbohydrate 7.5 g;
Fibre 2.3 g;
Fat 22 g/serving

1. Combine first 5 ingredients with half the olive oil and half the vinegar in a mini-chop or in a bowl using a handheld blender. Process until well combined but still rough in texture.
2. In a small cup, combine remaining oil and vinegar; whisk well to combine. Toss half this mixture in a bowl with the amount of greens you have chosen for 4 portions. There should be very little dressing – just a coating on the greens.
3. On each of 4 cold salad plates pile a small portion of dressed greens. Arrange alternating slices of tomato and Bocconcini on and around the greens, spreading the rough pesto mixture on the tomato slices as you work.
4. Drizzle the remaining oil and vinegar dressing over the top. Offer each plate with a pepper mill for cracked pepper, if desired.

PHOTO: JOHN SINAL

fresh crab and mango salad

MAKES 6 SERVINGS

1/3	cup [75 mL] very finely minced red onion
2	Tbsp. [30 mL] light mayonnaise
2	Tbsp. [30 mL] light sour cream
1/2	cup [125 mL] chopped and tightly packed fresh cilantro leaves, divided
1/4	cup [60 mL] fresh lime juice, divided
1	lb. [500 g] fresh crabmeat
1/2	cup [125 mL] olive oil
1-1/2	tsp. [8 mL] ground cumin
1	Tbsp. + 1 tsp. [20 mL] red wine or sherry vinegar
1	tsp. [5 mL] very finely minced Jalapeño pepper
6	cups [1.5 L] mixed salad greens, washed and torn into bite-size pieces
2	avocados, peeled, pitted, cut into 1/2" [1.25 cm] pieces
2	mangoes, peeled, pitted, cut into 1/2" [1.25 cm] pieces
1	small red bell pepper, seeded, very thinly sliced
1	lime, cut into 6 wedges, for garnish
	Salt and freshly ground black pepper

1. In a medium bowl, combine red onion, mayonnaise, sour cream, 6 Tbsp. [90 mL] cilantro, and 3 Tbsp. [45 mL] lime juice. Stir well to combine. Season to taste with salt and pepper and gently fold in the crabmeat.

2. In a small bowl, combine the remaining cilantro and lime juice, olive oil, cumin, vinegar and minced Jalapeño. Mix well to combine and season with salt and pepper. Toss the salad greens with half of the vinaigrette and place on 6 chilled salad plates.

3. Divide the crab between the 6 salads, mounding it in the centre of the salad.

4. Toss mangoes, avocados and pepper with remaining vinaigrette and arrange on the salads, surrounding the crab. Garnish with the lime wedges. Serve immediately.

Calories: 329;
Protein 15 g;
Carbohydrate 19 g;
Fibre 8 g;
Fat 22 g/serving

PHOTO: JOANNE FACCHIN

beet and pear salad

MAKES 6 SERVINGS

6	medium beets, cooked, peeled, diced, cooled
1/2	cup [125 mL] plain low-fat yogurt
2	Tbsp. [30 mL] liquid honey
1	tsp. [5 mL] Dijon mustard
1/8	tsp. [0.5 mL] grated nutmeg
2	Tbsp. [30 mL] chopped fresh mint
	Grated peel and juice of 1 orange
6	large leaf-lettuce leaves
2	Bartlett or Anjou pears, cored
	Salt and pepper
	Watercress sprigs

Calories: 105;
Protein 2.6 g;
Carbohydrate 25 g;
Fibre 4.6 g;
Fat 0.5 g/serving

1. Prepare beets and place in a large bowl.
2. In a small bowl, combine yogurt, honey, mustard, nutmeg, mint, orange peel and juice, salt and pepper to taste. Pour yogurt dressing over beets; mix well.
3. Arrange 1 lettuce leaf on each of 6 salad plates. Spoon beet mixture over top of lettuce.
4. Thinly slice pears. Arrange pear slices and watercress sprigs on top of beet mixture and serve.

cold asparagus salad

MAKES 4 ENTRÉE OR 8 APPETIZER SERVINGS

1	bunch fresh asparagus, trimmed, cut in 1.5" [3.75 cm] pieces
1	small red bell pepper, seeded, julienned
1	small yellow bell pepper, seeded, julienned
1	red onion, diced
1	[200 g] tub Bocconcini, drained*
	Lettuce leaves, spinach leaves or Belgian endive leaves

Dressing:

2	tsp. [10 mL] minced garlic and jalapeño**
2	Tbsp. [30 mL] Balsamic vinegar with raspberry juice
4	Tbsp. [60 mL] julienned sun-dried tomatoes, drained of oil
1	Tbsp. [15 mL] extra virgin olive oil
2	Tbsp. [30 mL] oil from sun-dried tomatoes
1	tsp. [5 mL] coarse black pepper
1/2	tsp. [3 mL] salt

Fresh Mozzarella cheese balls available in tubs in the deli section.
**Available in small jars in the produce section.*

---

1. Drop the asparagus pieces into salted boiling water for 1-2 minutes. Remove with a slotted spoon to a bowl of ice water.

2. Combine cold asparagus, red and yellow pepper strips and red onion in a large bowl. Refrigerate.

3. Combine dressing ingredients in a small bowl and whisk [or use an electric mixer or a hand-held blender] until well combined [do not overmix; the sun-dried tomato strips should remain whole].

4. Cut each Bocconcini ball into 4 pieces and place in a small bowl. Pour the dressing over and mix well. Cover and let stand at room temperature about 1 hour.

5. Add Bocconcini and dressing to the large bowl of vegetables and toss well. Line cold dinner plates or luncheon plates with the chosen greens and divide the dressed salad mixture among the plates. Serve at once.

Calories: 288;
Protein 15 g;
Carbohydrate 15 g;
Fibre 2 g;
Fat 20 g/entrée serving

spinach and apple salad
with poppy seed dressing

MAKES 8 SERVINGS

Poppy Seed Dressing:

1/4	cup [60 mL]	raspberry vinegar or red wine vinegar
1/4	cup [60 mL]	canola oil
1/4	cup [60 mL]	water
1	Tbsp. [15 mL]	granulated sugar
2	tsp. [10 mL]	poppy seeds
1/4	tsp. [1 mL]	paprika
1/4	tsp. [1 mL]	Worcestershire sauce
1		green onion, minced

Salad:

1/3	cup [75 mL]	sliced almonds
1/4	cup [60 mL]	granulated sugar
2	tsp. [10 mL]	water
1	lb. [500 g]	spinach [or 2 large bunches]
2		medium apples, cored, sliced
1	Tbsp. [15 mL]	freshly squeezed lemon juice

Calories: 193;
Protein 4.1 g;
Carbohydrate 18.5 g;
Fibre 2 g;
Fat 12.8 g/serving

1. To prepare dressing, in a jar combine all dressing ingredients and mix well.

2. Place almonds, sugar and water in a non-stick skillet. Using a wooden spoon, stir slowly over medium heat until sugar melts and almonds are coated and golden, about 6-8 minutes. Immediately remove almonds to a plate.

3. When cool, break into small pieces.

4. Just before serving, trim [discard tough stems], wash and dry spinach; tear into bite-size pieces. Place in salad bowl and set aside.

5. Add lemon juice to apple slices to prevent browning and set aside. Just before serving, pour dressing over spinach and toss to coat. Add apples and almonds and toss together. Serve immediately.

wild greens with raspberry dressing

MAKES 6 TO 8 SERVINGS

10	cups [2.5 L] washed, dried mixed baby and wild greens
2-1/2	cups [625 mL] fresh raspberries
	Cracked black pepper to serve

Dressing:

1	cup [250 mL] fresh raspberries
1/2	ripe papaya, peeled, seeded
1/3	cup [75 mL] Balsamic Vinegar with Raspberry Juice
1/3	cup [75 mL] extra virgin olive oil
1/2	tsp. [3 mL] ground cardamom
1	tsp. [5 mL] granulated sugar
	Salt and pepper, to taste

1. Combine all dressing ingredients in a food processor or in a bowl with a handheld blender. Process until smooth [if you prefer the dressing without raspberry seeds, push the dressing through a sieve at this point].

2. Dressing and greens can be refrigerated separately until serving time. When ready to serve, toss greens with desired amount of dressing, adding the raspberries at the last moment before serving.

3. Sprinkle salad with cracked pepper.

Note: This dressing would be fine for any salad, but is best with soft baby and wild greens rather than crisp lettuces like iceberg.

*Calories: 142;
Protein 1.7 g;
Carbohydrate 13 g;
Fibre 6 g;
Fat 10 g/serving*

PHOTO: JOHN SINAL

tabbouleh salad

MAKES 6 SERVINGS

1	cup [250 mL] bulgur wheat
2	cups [500 mL] boiling water
1	bunch green onions, chopped
2	ripe tomatoes, seeded, diced
1	cup [250 mL] chopped fresh parsley
1/2	cup [125 mL] packed chopped fresh mint
1	bunch radishes, sliced
1 1/2	tsp. [8 mL] salt
1/2	tsp. [3 mL] black pepper
3	garlic cloves, minced
1/4	cup [60 mL] fresh lemon juice
	Grated peel of 2 lemons
1/4	cup [60 mL] extra virgin olive oil

Calories: 184;
Protein 3.8 g;
Carbohydrate 23 g;
Fibre 4.2 g;
Fat 9.6 g/serving

1. Combine the bulgur wheat and boiling water in a medium bowl; let stand 20 minutes. Fluff with a fork and place in a sieve to drain all remaining water. Place in a large salad bowl.
2. Add next 5 ingredients and toss. Refrigerate until ready to serve.
3. To make the dressing, combine salt, pepper, garlic, lemon juice, peel and oil in a bowl with a handheld blender or in a blender or food processor. Process until smooth and slightly thickened.
4. Pour over salad and toss well to serve. If transporting to a picnic or party, pack the finished salad in a covered bowl, but pack the dressing and salad separately if you don't plan to serve it within an hour.

PHOTO: RAEFF MILES

layered vegetable salad
MAKES 10 SERVINGS

4	cups [1 L] finely chopped dark-green lettuce [such as romaine or mixed greens]
2-3	ripe tomatoes, diced
1	cup [250 mL] seeded, diced green bell peppers
1	cup [250 mL] grated Cheddar or Mozzarella cheese
1	cup [250 mL] thinly sliced celery
2	cups [500 mL] frozen green peas, thawed
1/2	cup [125 mL] chopped green onion
1/2	cup [125 mL] cooked and crumbled bacon [optional]
1	cup [250 mL] light mayonnaise
1	cup [250 mL] fat-free sour cream

1. Arrange lettuce as first layer in the bottom of the bowl.

2. Cover with a layer of tomatoes, then green peppers.

3. Top with a layer of grated cheese, followed by a layer of sliced celery.

4. Follow with a layer of peas. [Cooking the peas is not required.]

5. Combine mayonnaise and sour cream. Spread over the layer of peas.

6. Sprinkle with green onions and bacon, if using, as the final layer. Refrigerate until serving time. This salad can be made up to 1 day before serving.

Optional additional layers: The sky's the limit! Try chopped marinated artichoke hearts, frozen corn, red pepper slices, chopped cucumber, fresh or canned mushroom slices, lean meat cubes like ham or turkey, and different varieties of cheese.

Calories: 215;
Protein 7.1 g;
Carbohydrate 13.3 g;
Fibre 1.3 g;
Fat 15.4 g/serving

[meat & poultry]

Grilled Jerk Chicken
Chicken Pie in a Flash
Whole Roast Chicken with Chili Baste
Turkey Piccata
Pesto Turkey Pizza
Chicken Wellington Stuffed with Pesto
Fast Track Turkey Lemon Risotto
Saltspring Butterflied Leg of Lamb
Spice Crusted Roast Turkey
Italian Lamb Shanks
Roast Prime Rib with Garlic Herb Crust and Dumplings
Enchilada Casserole with Spiced Beef Filling
Beef and Mushroom Strudel
Barbecued Dry Ribs
Beef Daube with Wild Mushrooms
Louisiana Gumbo
Marinated Crown Roast of Pork with Fruit Stuffing
Autumn Apple and Pork Gratin
Crusty Baked Chops with Mustard
Pork Tenderloin with Sweet Sauce and Rice

grilled jerk chicken

MAKES SEASONING FOR 5 LB. [2.25 KG] CHICKEN [4 TO 5 SERVINGS]

5	bunches green onions, chopped
3	garlic cloves, chopped
3	Scotch Bonnet chilies, minced
2	sprigs fresh thyme
1	tsp. [5 mL] grated lime peel
1/4	cup [60 mL] ground allspice
2	Tbsp. [30 mL] ground pepper
1	Tbsp. [15 mL] granulated sugar
1-1/2	Tbsp. [25 mL] salt

*Calories: 94.1;
Protein 2.8 g;
Carbohydrate 24.1 g;
Fibre 0 g;
Fat 1.9 g/1 Tbsp.
[15 mL] of seasoning*

*Calories: 224;
Protein 30 g;
Carbohydrate 24 g;
Fibre 0 g;
Fat 3 g/serving of
chicken*

1. Combine all ingredients in a food processor or in a bowl with a handheld blender; blend to a paste consistency. Transfer the jerk paste to a well-sealed jar and keep refrigerated until ready to use. [Can be refrigerated for 2-3 days.]

2. To jerk chicken, use 1-2 tsp. [5-10 mL] of jerk seasoning paste and mix well with an equal amount of vegetable oil. Rub the jerk mixture into and under the chicken skin and marinate in refrigerator for at least 1 hour before grilling/barbecuing slowly at a medium temperature. If using a gas barbecue, place temperature at lowest gas point. If using barbecue briquettes, fire up a regular barbecue and cook the meat when the coals are all white.

chicken pie in a flash

MAKES 4 SERVINGS

3	tsp. [15 mL] vegetable oil, divided
8	chicken thighs or 2 whole chicken breasts, boned, skinned, cut into 1" [2.5 cm] chunks
1	onion, chopped
2	carrots, chunked
3/4	cup [175 mL] chicken broth
2-3	Tbsp. [30-45 mL] grainy mustard*
3/4	cup [175 mL] light cream
2	Tbsp. [30 mL] instant flour**
3/4	cup [175 mL] frozen peas
1/2	[397 g] pkg. frozen puff pastry, thawed in fridge
	Salt and pepper

*Any grainy/old-fashioned/whole mustard seed product will do.
**Regular all-purpose flour can be substituted but we find instant flour is an excellent product to keep in the kitchen. It is particularly useful for quick thickening needs like this since it will not lump when you stir it into the recipe.

---

1. Preheat oven to 400°F [200°C]. In a large skillet, heat 2 tsp. [10 mL] oil; when hot, add chicken chunks; sauté on all sides until browned; remove with a slotted spoon.
2. Add remaining oil to skillet and heat; when hot, add onion and carrots; sauté vegetables until partially cooked; add broth and chicken chunks and cover. Cook over medium heat about 10 minutes or until vegetables are just tender.
3. Meanwhile, roll one-half of the thawed puff pastry to approximately 12" [30 cm] square. Cut into 4 squares; cut each square diagonally into two and place on a cookie sheet. Bake about 13-15 minutes or until squares are puffed and golden brown. Keep warm while you finish the filling.
4. Combine mustard, cream and flour; mix well; add to skillet, stirring constantly over medium heat until mixture thickens slightly. Add peas, reduce heat to low and simmer until peas are tender. Taste sauce, season with salt and pepper, if desired.
5. To serve, divide filling among 4 shallow soup or pasta bowls and top each with two pastry triangles.

Calories: 537;
Protein 36 g;
Carbohydrate 34 g;
Fibre 3 g;
Fat 28 g/serving

chicken

whole roast chicken with chili baste

MAKES 6 SERVINGS

1	large roasting chicken [about 6 lbs./3 kg]*
2	Tbsp. [30 mL] ground cumin
1	large lemon, quartered
1	green bell pepper, seeded, quartered
1	medium onion, minced
4	garlic cloves, minced
2-3	chipotle peppers [in adobo sauce], minced**
3	Tbsp. [45 mL] minced fresh cilantro
1/2	tsp. [3 mL] salt
1	tsp. [5 mL] coarse black pepper
1	Tbsp. [15 mL] olive oil

*Or a small turkey or two smaller roasting chickens [reduce cooking time and divide chile mixture between the two birds].
**Available in tins in the Mexican foods section.

*Calories: 197;
Protein 25 g;
Carbohydrate 5.7 g;
Fibre 1.3 g;
Fat 7.9 g/serving
without skin*

1. Preheat oven to 350°F [180°C]. Spray a large roasting pan and place a rack in the centre.
2. Wash and thoroughly dry the chicken [save any giblets, neck, etc. for stock and gravy if desired]. Use your fingers to loosen the breast skin as far down to the wings and thighs as possible. Insert your fingers up under the skin on the thighs as well.
3. Sprinkle the cumin over the chunks of lemon and green pepper; place the chunks inside the bird's cavity.
4. Mix together the remaining 7 ingredients [use a food processor if possible]. Include some of the adobo sauce from the can as well as the chipotle chilies. Use your fingers to insert and spread this mixture underneath the skin – over the breast and up onto the thighs. Smooth the skin over top.
5. Use skewers and/or kitchen string to truss the bird securely. Press small pieces of foil over the top of each drumstick to prevent it from drying out. Place bird on the rack in the roasting pan. Place a large, loose tent of foil over the entire bird. Roast about 2 hours.
6. Remove the foil tent and the smaller pieces of foil from the legs. Baste. Return to the oven for another 45 minutes or until a meat thermometer reads 180°F [90°C], or the juices run clear when the meat is pricked with a fork or knife point.
7. Let stand on counter 10 minutes before carving. Remove lemon and green pepper chunks and string before placing on a serving platter.

turkey piccata

MAKES 4 TO 6 SERVINGS

1 – 1-1/2	lbs. [500-750 g] scaloppini-style turkey breast fillets
3	Tbsp. [45 mL] butter
3	Tbsp. [45 mL] vegetable oil
2	tsp. [10 mL] minced garlic
1/3	cup [75 mL] minced onion
1/4	cup [60 mL] dry white wine
3/4	cup [175 mL] chicken broth
	Grated peel and juice of 1 large lemon
2	tsp. [10 mL] Dijon mustard
3	Tbsp. [45 mL] drained capers
1/3	cup [75 mL] minced fresh parsley
	All-purpose flour
	Salt and pepper

1. Dip the turkey fillets into a mixture of flour, salt and pepper, shaking off excess.
2. Heat butter and oil in a large skillet. When hot, add turkey fillets and sauté over medium-high heat very quickly on both sides, removing them as they start to turn golden brown. Keep warm on a plate in a warm oven.
3. When all turkey pieces are sautéed, add garlic and onion to pan and cook until slightly softened.
4. Add wine to the hot pan to deglaze it, scraping up all the browned bits from the bottom of the pan. Reduce heat slightly and add chicken broth, peel, juice and mustard. Stir and heat for 1 minute.
5. Return turkey pieces to the pan. Add capers and parsley. Toss to coat all turkey pieces and serve at once with cracked pepper over top.

*Calories: 270;
Protein 25 g;
Carbohydrate 2.8 g;
Fibre 0.3 g;
Fat 16 g/serving*

pesto turkey pizza

MAKES 1 INDIVIDUAL PIZZA

1	[8"/20 cm] flour tortilla
2	Tbsp. [30 mL] pesto sauce*
3-4	Tbsp. [45-60 mL] diced cooked turkey
1	Tbsp. [15 mL] chopped black olives
2	Tbsp. [30 mL] chopped seeded tomato
1	Tbsp. [15 mL] chopped green onion
1/3	cup [75 mL] grated 4-cheese mix**
	Coarse black pepper

*Homemade or commercial pesto [we used a 170 mL pkg. of Western Family Pesto].
**This is a mixture of four grated cheeses – found in a resealable poly bag in the dairy section.

Calories: 451;
Protein 24 g;
Carbohydrate 19 g;
Fibre 1.5 g;
Fat 31 g/pizza

1. Preheat oven to 350°F [180°C].
2. Place tortilla on a baking sheet. Cover with ingredients in the order listed. Bake about 20 minutes or until hot and bubbly, with the cheese melted.
3. Cut into wedges and serve at once.

Note: These individual pizzas may be made up to 1 hour ahead of baking.

Nutrition note: White turkey meat is very lean containing only 115 calories and one gram of fat per 3-1/2 oz. (100g) serving. That's 10 per cent less than in a comparable serving of white chicken meat.

chicken wellington stuffed with pesto

MAKES 4 SERVINGS

2	whole boneless chicken breasts, skinned
4	large whole basil leaves or sprigs*
	Pastry for a double-crust pie
1	egg, beaten

Pesto:

1	cup [250 mL] packed basil leaves*
1/3	cup [75 mL] pine nuts
1/3	cup [75 mL] grated Parmesan cheese
1/4	cup [60 mL] extra-virgin olive oil
4	garlic cloves, halved
	Salt and pepper to taste

Use either the small plastic packages [available in the produce department] or the fresh leaves direct from basil plants.

---

1. To prepare pesto: Combine all ingredients in a food processor or mini-chopper. Process until well-combined and thick. Refrigerate until ready to use [will keep up to 5 days in refrigerator].

2. Preheat oven to 425°F [210°C]. Dry the chicken breasts and cut in half, trimming off any fat or sinews. Make a cut into the meat splitting each half in half again horizontally; do not cut all the way through – just far enough to enable you to lay the halves open on the counter.

3. Place 2 Tbsp. [30 mL] of the pesto in the cut of each breast half, spreading evenly over the meat; fold the chicken meat over the pesto to enclose.

4. Cut pastry into four equal lumps; roll each piece of pastry out on a floured board into a rectangle about 8" [20 cm] long and 7" [18 cm] wide. [Size will depend on the size of your breast halves. Make the rectangles about 1/2"/1.25 cm longer than the piece of chicken on each end.]

5. Place one large basil leaf or sprig in the centre of each rectangle. Invert a stuffed chicken piece over the leaf. Use the beaten egg with a soft brush to brush the long edges of the pastry; bring up around the chicken and seal together. Trim the rectangle ends and use egg wash to also seal those together. Invert [so basil leaf is now on top] and place each on an ungreased baking sheet.

6. Roll out any pastry trimmings and cut leaves for decoration. Egg wash the outside of each Wellington; egg wash the leaves and other decorations onto the tops.

7. Place in oven for 20 minutes or until pastry is browned; reduce heat to 350°F [180°C]. Bake for another 30 minutes [for larger breast halves; slightly less for small ones].

8. Serve with a salad or green vegetable.

Calories: 716;
Protein 37 g;
Carbohydrate 34 g;
Fibre 0 g;
Fat 48 g/serving

fast track turkey lemon risotto

MAKES 4 TO 6 ENTREE SERVINGS

4	slices lean bacon
1	large onion, minced
4	garlic cloves, minced
1-1/2	cups [375 mL] Arborio [short grain] or pearl rice
4	[10 fl. oz./284 mL] tins boiling chicken broth
2	cups [500 mL] diced cooked turkey
1/2	tsp. [3 mL] coarse black pepper
1	Tbsp. [15 mL] chopped fresh tarragon
	Grated peel and juice of 1 large lemon
1	ripe tomato, seeded, chopped [optional]

Calories: 451;
Protein 41 g;
Carbohydrate 56 g;
Fibre 2 g;
Fat 7 g/serving

1. In a large saucepan cook the bacon until crisp; remove from pan; chop and set aside.
2. In the fat that is left in the pan, sauté the onion and garlic until the onion is slightly soft.
3. Add rice and mix well to coat rice grains with the bacon fat.
4. Add the boiling chicken broth [easy to do in the microwave while cooking the onion]. Stir to mix well; reduce heat to a strong simmer; cover. Cook about 20 minutes or until mixture is a creamy consistency [it should not be stiff – more soupy in texture].
5. Add diced bacon, cooked turkey, pepper, tarragon, lemon peel and juice and tomato [if using]. Mix well and cook another 5 minutes until heated through.

Serving suggestion: Serve risotto in heated shallow bowls with crisp flatbread and a crisp slaw or salad.

Note: Risottos are very loose and creamy mixtures – achieved by having the rice absorb liquids of various kinds over heat for a long period of time. By boiling the broth first, you shortcut the process and put dinner on the table in half the time!

fast track
turkey
risotto

saltspring
butterflied
leg of
lamb

saltspring butterflied leg of lamb

MAKES 4 TO 5 SERVINGS

3	Tbsp. [45 mL] olive oil
2	tsp. [10 mL] minced garlic
1	Tbsp. [15 mL] dried tarragon leaves, crushed
4-5	lb. [2-2.5 kg] leg of lamb, boned, butterflied
3	Tbsp. [45 mL] Dijon mustard, divided
1/3	cup [75 mL] grated Parmesan cheese
2	Tbsp. [30 mL] chopped fresh parsley
2	Tbsp. [30 mL] fine dry bread crumbs
2	Tbsp. [30 mL] butter, melted
	Fresh mint or tarragon sprigs

1. In a small bowl, mix together oil, garlic and tarragon; brush over all sides of the lamb. Let stand at room temperature for 3 hours, turning once.

2. Preheat broiler. Place meat in a shallow baking dish. Brush with one-half of the mustard; broil 3" [7.5 cm] from source of heat for 5 minutes; brush with remaining mustard. Broil for 4 minutes.

3. Turn oven temperature to "bake" at 450°F [230°C]. In a small bowl mix together cheese, parsley, bread crumbs and melted butter. Pat gently over meat surface. Roast until thermometer inserted in the thickest portion of the meat reads 130°F [65°C] for rare, and the crumbs are crisp and browned.

4. Let stand 10 minutes before carving into thin slices.

5. To serve, garnish platter with fresh mint sprigs.

Note: The lamb can be marinated in the refrigerator for up to 3 days, then cooked on the day of serving. In fact, the flavour will improve the longer it stays in the marinade.

Calories: 710;
Protein 87 g;
Carbohydrate 10 g;
Fibre 0.2 g;
Fat 34 g/serving

spice crusted roast turkey

MAKES 6 SERVINGS [WITH LEFTOVERS]

Spice Paste:

6	garlic cloves, peeled
1	large shallot, peeled
1	fresh chili pepper, Serrano or Jalapeño, seeded
1	Tbsp. [15 mL] ground cumin
1	Tbsp. [15 mL] ground coriander
2	tsp. [10 mL] turmeric
2	tsp. [10 mL] Madras curry powder
1	tsp. [5 mL] fennel seed
1	tsp. [5 mL] salt
1	tsp. [5 mL] freshly ground black pepper
1/4	cup [60 mL] vegetable oil
3	Tbsp. [45 mL] fresh lime juice
1	[10 lb./5 kg] fresh whole turkey
1/2	cup [125 mL] dry white wine
1	cup [250 mL] chicken or turkey broth

Calories: 210;
Protein 28 g;
Carbohydrate 1.8 g;
Fibre 0 g;
Fat 9 g/serving

1. In the bowl of a food processor, combine the garlic, shallot and fresh chili. Process until very finely chopped. Add the cumin, coriander, turmeric, Madras curry powder, fennel seed, salt and pepper. Purée the spices with the garlic mixture. Add the oil and process until a smooth paste is formed.

2. Transfer the paste to a small non-stick skillet and cook over medium heat, stirring, until fragrant and toasted, 3-4 minutes. Allow to cool and stir in lime juice.

3. Place the turkey on a large cutting board and pat dry with paper towels. Loosen the skin of the bird using your fingers and separate skin from the breast and thighs. Spread 1/2 of the spice paste under the skin over the breast and thighs of the bird. Spread the remaining paste over the entire bird, including the cavity, rubbing it thoroughly into the skin. Season generously with salt and pepper. Truss the turkey, fold in wing tips and place in a roasting pan. Cover loosely with plastic wrap and refrigerate for up to 24 hours.

4. Preheat oven to 375°F [190°C]. Pour the wine and broth into the roasting pan and roast the turkey for 45 minutes.

5. Baste the turkey with the pan juices, lower the oven temperature to 350°F [180°C] and continue cooking about 3 hours, basting the turkey every half hour. The turkey is cooked when a meat thermometer inserted into the fattest part of the thigh registers 180°F [85°C].

6. Transfer the turkey to a platter and allow to stand for 30 minutes before carving.

7. Strain pan juices into a large measuring cup; skim off all visible fat. Transfer to a saucepan. Bring to a boil then reduce heat to medium and simmer until reduced by half. Season with salt and pepper and strain into a sauce boat.

8. Serve the turkey with the sauce and a cranberry chutney.

italian lamb shanks

MAKES 4 SERVINGS

4	lamb shanks, thawed if frozen
	Olive oil
1	cup [250 mL] dry white wine
1	cup [250 mL] strong beef stock
2	large onions, chopped
2	plum tomatoes, chopped
2	medium carrots, peeled, sliced into rounds
1	celery stalk, sliced on an angle
1	tsp. [5 mL] minced garlic
1	tsp. [5 mL] ground marjoram
1	tsp. [5 mL] salt
2	Tbsp. [30 mL] cornstarch
2	Tbsp. [30 mL] cold water
2	Tbsp. [30 mL] fresh chopped parsley
	Grated peel of 1 lemon
1	tsp. [5 mL] mashed garlic
	Hot cooked noodles or risotto
	Pepper, to taste
	Water

1. Preheat oven to 400°F [200°C].
2. Remove fat from shanks; brush on all sides with olive oil; place in a single layer in a 9" x 13" [23 cm x 32.5 cm] baking dish. Roast, uncovered, for 35 minutes until meat is browned; turn shanks over.
3. Reduce oven temperature to 300°F [150°C].
4. Combine wine and beef stock; heat on top of stove or in microwave until hot; pour over shanks.
5. Add vegetables, garlic, marjoram, salt and pepper to dish; cover dish with aluminum foil. Roast for 2 to 2-1/2 hours, until meat is so tender it pulls apart easily.
6. Remove meat and vegetables to centre of a serving platter; keep warm. Pour liquid left in dish into a measuring cup; add water to make 2 cups [500 mL]; return liquid to dish; bring to boil in microwave [or transfer to saucepan and heat on stove].
7. Blend cornstarch and cold water; add a little of hot liquid; stir to blend; return all to dish or saucepan; stir and cook or microwave until sauce is thick.
8. Combine parsley, lemon peel and garlic to make a paste.
9. To serve, surround meat and vegetables on platter with hot cooked noodles or risotto. Top with parsley mixture and pour sauce over all.

Calories: 460;
Protein 20 g;
Carbohydrate 15 g;
Fibre 4.3 g;
Fat 30 g/serving

roast prime rib with garlic herb crust & dumplings

MAKES 8 TO 10 SERVINGS

1	3-rib prime rib roast [about 6 lbs./3 kg]

Crust:

1/2	cup [125 mL] fine dry bread crumbs
6	Tbsp. [90 mL] minced garlic*
4	Tbsp. [60 mL] creamed horseradish
2	Tbsp. [30 mL] minced fresh oregano
2	Tbsp. [30 mL] minced fresh rosemary
2	Tbsp. [30 mL] minced fresh sage
2	Tbsp. [30 mL] minced fresh parsley
1	tsp. [5 mL] coarse black pepper
2	Tbsp. [30 mL] olive oil
4	large baking potatoes

Dumplings:

2	cups [500 mL] all-purpose flour
3/4	cup [175 mL] finely ground suet [found frozen, can be used frozen]
1	tsp. [5 mL] salt
1/2	[2 mL] coarse black pepper
1	Tbsp. [15 mL] baking powder
2	Tbsp. [30 mL] minced fresh herbs [mixture of the ones used in the crust]
3/4-1	cup [175-250 mL] cold water**

*Small jars of minced garlic can be found in the produce department.
**The amount of water may vary according to the warmth of your hands and the kitchen.

Calories: 902;
Protein 77 g;
Carbohydrate 45 g;
Fibre 2.8 g;
Fat 46 g/serving

1. Preheat oven to 400°F [200°C]. Trim all visible fat from the roast; make sure it is tied with string to an even thickness.

2. In a large bowl, combine all crust ingredients; mix well. Press firmly all over the outer surface of the roast, smoothing evenly and pressing into place. Place on small rack in a large roasting pan. Place a loose tent of foil over the roast. Place in centre of oven. Reduce heat at once to 350°F [180°C]. Roast until meat thermometer shows internal temperature is 140°F [60°C] for rare, usually about 25 minutes per lb. [500 g].

3. One hour and 15 minutes before the roasting is due to finish, peel and cut potatoes into thirds or quarters. Par-boil until only half-cooked. Drain well.

4. Check for fat in the bottom of the roaster from the meat. If not, add a little vegetable oil to the pan bottom. Let heat 5 minutes. When very hot, add potatoes to pan, turning each piece to coat with the oil. Remove the foil tent and continue roasting.

5. To make the dumplings: Combine all ingredients except water in a medium bowl. Slowly add water, mixing with your hands and gently pulling dough together to form a soft but not sticky dough. [All the water may or may not be needed.]

6. About 20 minutes from roasting completion, turn potato pieces again. Divide dumpling dough into 8 small balls. Drop into the hot fat among the potato pieces. After 15 minutes, turn dumplings over. When roasting is complete, potatoes and dumplings should be browned and crispy on all sides.

enchilada casserole with spiced beef filling

MAKES 6 TO 8 SERVINGS

1	lb. [500 g] boneless lean beef chuck, diced
2	cups [500 mL] water
1	tsp. [5 mL] salt
1	small onion, chunked
1	Tbsp. [15 mL] vegetable oil
3	garlic cloves, minced
1	small onion, diced
1	green Japapeño pepper, seeded, minced
2	small tomatoes, seeded, diced
3/4	tsp. [4 mL] salt
1/2	tsp. [3 mL] black pepper
3/4	tsp. [4 mL] ground cumin
1/2	tsp. [3 mL] dried oregano leaves
2	Tbsp. [30 mL] minced mixed fresh herbs*
1/2	cup [125 mL] reserved beef cooking liquid
1	[700 mL] jar Healthy Choice [no-fat] Garlic Lovers Pasta Sauce
1	cup [250 mL] V8 juice
1/3	cup [75 mL] vegetable oil
1	[283 g] pkg. of 12 corn tortillas
1	cup [250 mL] grated Monterey Jack cheese with Jalapeños
1	cup [250 mL] grated "old" Cheddar cheese
	Sour cream [optional]
	Guacamole [optional]

*In the test kitchen we used a mixture of sage, oregano and thyme.

---

1. Combine the beef, water, salt and onion chunks in a small saucepan and cook, lid tilted, at a strong simmer for 1-1/2 hours. Drain and reserve cooking liquid. Use two forks to pull meat apart until it is all shredded. Place in a bowl.

2. Meanwhile, heat 1 Tbsp. [15 mL] oil in a small skillet. Sauté garlic, onion and Jalapeño over medium heat until softened.

3. Combine skillet contents with meat in the bowl. Stir in tomatoes, seasonings and the 1/2 cup [125 mL] reserved cooking liquid; set aside.

4. Preheat oven to 350°F [180°C]. Heat pasta sauce and V8 juice in a skillet.

5. Heat 1/3 cup [175 mL] oil in another skillet over medium heat. Using tongs [without serrated teeth on the ends], quickly dip the first corn tortilla in the oil, flip it over and remove [a total of no more than 2 seconds]. Then, just as quickly, dip both sides in the hot sauce; remove to a board or flat plate.

6. Spread a little of the meat mixture on one half of the tortilla and fold the other half over top. Place in a 9" x 12" [23 x 30 cm] baking dish. Continue with all the tortillas until all are filled and placed, overlapping, in the baking dish.

7. Discard oil in skillet. Pour hot sauce over the enchiladas, smoothing evenly to make sure all tortilla edges are covered. Sprinkle cheeses over top and bake 30 minutes or until bubbly. Let stand 10 minutes before serving with sour cream and guacamole.

*Calories: 675;
Protein 35.2 g;
Carbohydrate 47.8 g;
Fibre 4.5 g;
Fat 39.8 g/serving*

beef

beef and mushroom strudel

MAKES 4 SERVINGS

1/2	lb. [250 g] lean ground beef
2	Portobello mushrooms, diced
3	garlic cloves, minced
1	small onion, minced
4	Tbsp. [60 mL] tomato paste
1/3	cup [75 mL] chopped toasted pine nuts*
1/3	cup [75 mL] golden or dark raisins
1	tsp. [5 mL] ground allspice
1/4-1/2	tsp. [1-3 mL] ground cloves
1/2	tsp. [3 mL] salt
1/4	tsp. [1 mL] coarse black pepper
1/2	[397 g] pkg. frozen puff pastry, thawed
1	egg, beaten

*Toast nuts on a baking sheet in a 350°F [180°C] oven for about 8 minutes, until browned.

Calories: 576;
Protein 22.7 g;
Carbohydrate 70 g;
Fibre 2.6 g;
Fat 24 g/serving

1. Preheat oven to 400°F [200°C].

2. Combine first 11 ingredients in a medium bowl and mix well.

3. Roll out thawed pastry on a floured board to a rectangle approximately 10" x 13-1/2" [25 cm x 33.75 cm]. Place on a baking sheet, with the shorter 10" [25 cm] end towards you. Pile meat filling down the centre of the pastry rectangle, leaving uncovered about 2-1/2" [6.25 cm] pastry on each side and about 1-1/2" [3.75 cm] pastry at top and bottom. Slash both sides of the uncovered pastry 4 or 5 times at an angle up and away from you.

4. Brush the beaten egg over all uncovered pastry surfaces. Fold the top and bottom of the pastry rectangle up and over the filling. Then bring the side pieces up over the filling, alternating the right and left side strips produced from your slashes. When all pastry is up and over the filling [some filling will show through the slashes], brush the whole strudel with the beaten egg. Bake about 35 minutes or until strudel is browned and filling is bubbly. Let stand 5 minutes before slicing.

PHOTO: JOHN SHERLOCK

barbecued dry ribs

MAKES 4 SERVINGS

5-6	lbs. [2.25-2.75 kg] baby back ribs
2	[225 mL] jars Asian Family Honey Garlic Sauce
	Coarse salt*
	Cracked pepper

*Do not substitute regular salt.

---

1. Preheat oven to 400°F [200°C].

2. Trim excess fat from ribs and cut into one-bone sections. Place in a large shallow roaster or baker. Pour about 3 cups [750 mL] water over ribs and cover with foil. Bake about 45 minutes.

3. Drain well, pour honey garlic sauce over and turn all pieces until fully coated. Cover and marinate in fridge overnight. Stir occasionally to coat pieces with sauce.

4. Preheat barbecue to medium-low heat. Use tongs to place rib pieces on the grill. Discard remaining marinade. Turn after about 4 minutes. After another 4 minutes, remove and immediately toss with a generous amount of coarse salt and pepper.

5. Serve at once. Use your fingers!

Calories: 360;
Protein 35 g;
Carbohydrate 24 g;
Fibre 0 g;
Fat 13 g/serving

beef daube with wild mushrooms

MAKES 8 SERVINGS

Stew:

4	lbs. [2 kg] trimmed stewing beef
1	[0.75 oz./22 g] pkg. dried porcini mushrooms
1	cup [250 mL] boiling water
1/3	cup [75 mL] all-purpose flour
3	strips bacon, diced or 2 oz. [60 g] pancetta, diced
2	large carrots, peeled, coarsely chopped
1	large onion, chopped
3	whole tomatoes, peeled, chopped
1/4	cup [60 mL] pitted black calamata olives
1/4	tsp. [2 mL] salt
1/8	tsp. [1 mL] freshly ground black pepper
2	Tbsp. [30 mL] minced fresh parsley

Marinade:

2	large carrots, peeled, sliced into coins
1	large onion, sliced
2	garlic cloves, minced
1/4	cup [60 mL] chopped parsley
1"	[2.5 cm] strip of orange peel, white pith removed
1	[750 mL] bottle good-quality dry red wine
	Bouquet Garni*

Bouquet Garni is a collection of fresh herbs tied together or placed in cheesecloth and used to flavour soups, stews and broths. Here, tie together 1 large sprig rosemary, 6 fresh thyme sprigs and 2 bay leaves and add to marinade.

*Calories 575;
Protein 62 g;
Carbohydrate 16.5 g;
Fibre 2.9 g;
Fat 22.6 g/serving*

1. Cut beef into 2" [5 cm] chunks. Place in a large bowl. Add remaining marinade ingredients and stir in until evenly mixed. Submerge beef in liquid. Cover and marinate at room temperature for 2 hours or refrigerate overnight.
2. When meat has marinated, combine dried mushrooms and boiling water in a heat-proof bowl for about 20 minutes or until fully rehydrated. Stir gently to loosen any grit. Remove mushrooms, chop and set aside.
3. Allow grit in the water to settle, then strain liquid into a cup and reserve. Discard grit.
4. Remove beef cubes from marinade and place in a large bowl. Toss with flour until evenly coated. Set aside.
5. Sauté bacon or pancetta in a heavy-bottomed saucepan until crisp. Remove to a casserole dish large enough to hold all the stew ingredients.
6. Add carrots and onion to fat remaining in pan; sauté for 5 minutes or until carrots are tender-crisp and onion is translucent. Remove and add to bacon in casserole dish, alternating with layers of floured beef cubes. Fold in chopped porcini mushrooms, chopped tomatoes and olives. Strain marinade juices into saucepan, along with liquid from mushrooms. Discard marinade ingredients except for a sprig of rosemary and the orange peel, add to the meat. Boil marinade juices until reduced by half, 10 minutes.
7. Preheat oven to 325°F [160°C]. Strain marinade and pour over meat. Cover casserole tightly and place in the centre of the preheated oven. Bake for 3 hours or until beef cubes are very tender. Add salt and fresh pepper and sprinkle with minced parsley.

beef
daube

louisiana
gumbo

louisiana gumbo

MAKES 6 SERVINGS

3/4	cup [175 mL] vegetable oil
3/4	cup [175 mL] all-purpose flour
1	medium onion, finely chopped
1	medium green bell pepper, seeded, finely chopped
2	stalks celery, finely chopped
1/2	lb. [250 g] okra, rinsed, dried and cut into 1/2" [1.25 cm] chunks
2	garlic cloves, minced
1/3	cup [75 mL] chopped Italian parsley
1	lb. [500 g] chorizo sausage, cut into 1" [2.5 cm] pieces
6	chicken thighs
6	cups [1.5 L] hot chicken, beef or fish broth [or a combination]
1/4	cup [60 mL] Worcestershire sauce
1/2	tsp. [3 mL] Tabasco sauce, or to taste
1	tsp. [5 mL] salt
1/2	tsp. [3 mL] cayenne
1	cup [250 mL] chopped tinned tomatoes
1/2	tsp. [3 mL] dried thyme
1/2	tsp. [3 mL] dried rosemary
1/4	tsp. [2 mL] crushed red pepper flakes
1	cup [250 mL] cooked shredded chicken
1	lb. [500 g] medium prawns, peeled and deveined
1	pint [500 mL] shucked small oysters [optional]
1/2	lb. [250 g] crabmeat [optional]
	Hot cooked white rice
	Green onion or parsley, finely chopped

1. In a heavy soup pot or large saucepan, heat vegetable oil over medium-low heat. Whisk in flour and stir frequently for about 20 minutes, then stir constantly until the paste [or roux] is very dark brown, about 15 minutes longer. Watch carefully – do not allow the roux to burn.

2. Add the onion, green pepper, celery, okra, garlic, parsley, chorizo sausage and chicken thighs. Cook until the vegetables are soft and the sausage is cooked, 15-20 minutes.

3. Add the hot broth in a thin stream, stirring constantly. [Don't add the broth too quickly or at too low a temperature, or the roux will separate.]

4. Add the Worcestershire sauce, Tabasco sauce, salt, cayenne, tinned tomatoes, thyme, rosemary and chile flakes. Reduce to low, stirring frequently.

5. Cover and simmer for 1 hour.

6. To serve, add the shredded chicken, prawns, oysters and crabmeat [if using] and cook 3-5 minutes. Ladle gumbo into individual heated bowls and serve each with a scoop of hot white rice. Garnish with finely chopped green onion or parsley.

Calories: 888;
Protein 59 g;
Carbohydrate 26 g;
Fibre 3.5 g;
Fat 60 g/serving
[without oysters,
crabmeat or rice]

marinated crown roast of pork with fruit stuffing

MAKES 10 SERVINGS

6-8	lb. [3-4 kg] crown roast of pork
	Juice of 2 lemons
1	Tbsp. [15 mL] minced garlic
1	Tbsp. [15 mL] grated fresh ginger [or purchase minced ginger in a jar]
2	Tbsp. [30 mL] minced fresh rosemary
2	Tbsp. [30 mL] minced fresh sage
2	Tbsp. [30 mL] liquid honey
	Salt and pepper to taste

Stuffing:

12	pitted prunes
12	dried apricots
12	dried apple rings
1	cup [250 mL] boiling chicken broth
1	onion, diced
1-1/2	Tbsp. [25 mL] minced fresh rosemary
1-1/2	Tbsp. [25 mL] minced fresh sage
1	tsp. [5 mL] black pepper
1	tsp. [5 mL] salt
3/4	tsp. [4 mL] ground cinnamon
2	cups [500 mL] fresh whole-wheat bread crumbs

*Calories: 549;
Protein 67.7 g;
Carbohydrate 36.4 g;
Fibre 2.6 g;
Fat 13.7 g/serving*

1. Wipe the roast and place in a non-metallic baking dish. Combine the following 8 ingredients into a marinade and brush over the roast, making sure the mixture goes into the centre and into the chop cuts around the outside. Let stand 1 hour.

2. For the stuffing, combine the dried fruits in a bowl and cover with the boiling broth. Let stand 20 minutes. Drain liquid off into a small saucepan.

3. Chop fruit [not too small]; place in a large bowl. Add the onion, rosemary and sage to the broth and boil for 10 minutes. Add to dried fruit in bowl. Add pepper, salt, cinnamon and crumbs. Mix well.

4. Preheat oven to 350°F [180°C]. Place roast in a roasting pan [on a rack] and brush with any marinade that has dripped off it during its standing time.

5. Spoon stuffing into the middle of the roast, piling it high above the bones. Wrap any leftover stuffing in a small foil package. Cover top of stuffing in the roast with a piece of foil sprayed with vegetable oil cooking spray. Roast pork about 1 hour. Remove the foil.

6. Place the extra stuffing in the foil package in the oven with the roast. Continue roasting another 1/2-3/4 hour. Check internal temperature with an instant-read thermometer [or use a regular meat thermometer in the roast from the beginning] and make sure it is just under 160°F [75°C]. Do not overcook.

7. Remove roast from oven, cover with foil and let rest 10 minutes. [It will continue to cook while standing so do not worry if the internal temperature is a little under 160°F/75°C.] Serve with crisp roasted potatoes and a gratinéed blend of broccoli and cauliflower. If cooking the roast without stuffing, reduce the cooking time by about 1/2 hour.

autumn apple and pork gratin

MAKES 6 TO 8 SERVINGS

1	Tbsp. [15 mL] each butter and olive oil, divided
	Seasoned flour*
1	lb. [500 g] pork tenderloin, sliced into 1/4" [0.6 cm] strips
1/2	cup [125 mL] ale or dark lager beer
1	large onion, thinly sliced
2	garlic cloves, minced
1-1/2	cups [375 mL] 2% milk
1	cup [250 mL] chicken broth, ale or combination
2	Tbsp. [30 mL] Dijon mustard
5-6	medium potatoes, preferably Yukon Gold, peeled, thinly sliced
4-5	medium tart cooking apples, peeled, cored, thinly sliced
1/2	cup [125 mL] grated Gruyère cheese
1/4	cup [60 mL] minced fresh herbs [parsley, thyme, rosemary, tarragon, etc.]
	Freshly ground pepper

*Seasoned flour: Combine together in a shallow dish: 1/4 cup [60 mL] flour; 1 Tbsp. [15 mL] dry mustard powder; 1 tsp. [5 mL] each paprika and salt; 1 tsp. [5 mL] dried herbs or 1 Tbsp. [15 mL] minced fresh herbs. Thyme, tarragon, savory and rosemary are all good choices. Freshly ground pepper to taste.

---

1. Preheat oven to 375°F [190°C].

2. Melt 1 tsp. [5 mL] each butter and oil in a large, non-stick skillet over medium-high heat. Lightly dredge pork slices in seasoned flour [reserve leftover flour mixture]. Sauté 1 minute on each side until lightly browned [do not crowd], adding a little more butter and oil to the pan if needed. Keep cooked slices warm until all are cooked.

3. Add beer to pan; increase heat; boil 30 seconds; scrape brown bits and liquid into a small mixing bowl; reserve.

4. Add another 1 tsp. [5 mL] each butter and oil to hot pan; stir in onions and garlic; sauté over medium heat until lightly browned and translucent. Combine with pork and reserve.

5. Add milk, broth or ale, Dijon mustard and leftover seasoned flour to reserved liquid in bowl; whisk together until smooth; set aside.

6. Lightly grease or spray a 9" x 12" [23 x 30 cm] shallow baking dish. Layer ingredients in order given: 1/2 the potato slices, 1/2 the apple slices, reserved pork and onion slices, remaining 1/2 of the apples and remaining 1/2 of potatoes.

7. Whisk milk mixture again and pour evenly over the casserole. Cover tightly and bake 45 minutes.

8. Remove cover, sprinkle evenly with cheese and herbs, season with freshly ground pepper. Reduce oven temperature to 350°F [180°C] and continue baking until potatoes are fork tender and cheese is golden, about 15 minutes.

9. Remove from oven and let stand 5 minutes before serving. Serve with your favourite "micro-brew."

Calories: 454;
Protein 33 g;
Carbohydrate 47 g;
Fibre 4.4 g;
Fat 15 g/serving

PHOTO: JOHN SINAL

crusty baked chops with mustard

MAKES 4 SERVINGS

1	cup [250 mL] fresh white bread crumbs
2	Tbsp. [30 mL] minced fresh parsley
1/4	tsp. [1 mL] salt
1/4	cup [60 mL] dry mustard
2	Tbsp. [30 mL] liquid honey
4	[6 oz./180 g] centre-cut "Our Premium Tender Marinated Pork" chops, 3/4" [2 cm] thick
	Freshly ground black pepper

Calories: 410;
Protein 43 g;
Carbohydrate 31 g;
Fibre 1.1 g;
Fat 12 g/serving

1. Preheat oven to 350°F [180°C].

2. Lightly spray a 9" x 13" [23 x 32.5 cm] baking dish.

3. Combine fresh bread crumbs, parsley, salt and pepper in a shallow bowl. Stir to blend.

4. Combine mustard and honey in a small bowl and stir to blend. Brush mustard mixture over chops and roll in breadcrumb mixture pressing crumbs firmly into chops. Place in a single layer in baking dish, making sure chops aren't touching. Bake in the centre of oven for 35 minutes or until chops are cooked through.

5. Remove from the oven and preheat broiler. Lightly spray chops with a little cooking oil and return chops to the oven; broil until crust is golden, about 2 minutes.

pork tenderloin with sweet sauce and rice
MAKES 4 SERVINGS

1/4	cup [60 mL] dark soy sauce
3	Tbsp. [45 mL] dry red wine
3	Tbsp. [45 mL] packed brown sugar
2	Tbsp. [30 mL] liquid honey
3	garlic cloves, minced
3/4	tsp. [4 mL] chili powder
2-3	drops red food colouring [optional]
1	lb. [500 g] pork tenderloin
1-1/2	lb. [750 g] broccoli florets
2-1/2	cups [625 mL] tomato [or V8] juice
1	tsp. [5 mL] coarse black pepper
2	cups [500 mL] instant rice
1	bunch green onions, sliced

1. Mix together the first 7 ingredients in a large bowl.

2. Trim all visible fat from the pork and slice into small, thin strips. Add to the bowl; toss to coat all meat pieces. Cover and marinate on counter for up to 1 hour or in fridge up to 8 hours. [The longer it marinates, the better the flavour.]

3. Heat a wok to about 400°F [200°C]. Use a slotted spoon to remove the pork from the marinade and add to the hot wok. Stir-fry about 1 minute or until pork is half-cooked.

4. Add broccoli, mix and cover. Cook 1 minute; stir and remove both pork and broccoli from wok. Keep warm.

5. Reduce wok heat slightly and add the marinade. Stir in tomato [or V8] juice and pepper. Cover wok until liquid is boiling.

6. Stir in rice. Reduce heat to about 300°F [150°C]. Cover and cook 4-5 minutes.

7. Remove lid and stir rice [it should be cooked but still slightly sloppy].

8. Add pork, broccoli and green onion; stir-fry 1 minute, then serve.

Calories: 518;
Protein 42 g;
Carbohydrate 80 g;
Fibre 7.3 g;
Fat 4.1 g/serving

[fish & shellfish]

Gingered Sole Rolls on a Vegetable Bed

Broccoli Sole Packets

Tomato Prawn Pizza

Snapper Veracruz

Barbecued Salmon with Lemon, Capers and Orzo

Parmesan Crusted Halibut

Seafood Stuffed Portobellos

Wok Fried Crab with Ginger and Black Beans

Grilled Bass with Roasted Garlic Citrus Baste

Chilled Salmon with Watercress Sauce

Halibut in White Wine with Rosemary

Classic Prawn Newburg

Herbed Seafood Stew

Fiery Prawn Wok

Tuna Souvlakia

Steamed Mussels and Clams with Coconut Milk and Lemon Grass

gingered sole rolls on a vegetable bed

MAKES 4 SERVINGS

1/4	lb. [125 g] machine-peeled shrimp, coarsely chopped
2	tsp. [10 mL] grated fresh ginger root
2	Tbsp. [30 mL] minced cilantro
3	garlic cloves, minced or puréed
2	Tbsp. [30 mL] white wine vinegar
4	thick sole fillets
1	Tbsp. [15 mL] olive oil
4	cups [1 L] mixed julienned vegetables*
4	Tbsp. [60 mL] sherry
3/4	cup [175 mL] whipping cream
	Chopped cilantro [optional]

* Choose a selection of your favourite vegetables [carrots, celery, green onion, leeks, zucchini, etc.] and cut the julienne strips quite thin.

Calories: 444;
Protein 43 g;
Carbohydrate 23 g;
Fibre 5.7 g;
Fat 20 g/serving

1. Combine first 5 ingredients in a small bowl; mix well.
2. Place sole fillets on the counter, underside up. Divide shrimp mixture among them and spread evenly over each fillet. Roll up fillets; place in a small buttered or sprayed baking dish so the rolls stay close together. Brush rolls with olive oil.
3. Preheat broiler. Place julienned vegetables in a small microwave-proof casserole; sprinkle with the sherry; cover loosely with plastic wrap. Microwave on high [100%] power about 4-5 minutes or until just tender.
4. Drain off liquid, reserving 1/4 cup [60 mL]. Replace wrap on vegetable dish to keep warm.
5. Combine reserved cooking liquid with cream in a small shallow skillet over high heat. Boil until reduced by half and slightly thickened.
6. Meanwhile, place sole rolls about 3"-4" [7.5-10 cm] from broiler; broil about 5-7 minutes, depending on thickness. Serve vegetables on a warm platter, topped with sole rolls. Drizzle sauce over top.

Serving suggestion: Serve with roasted garlic smashed potatoes.

broccoli sole packets

MAKES 4 SERVINGS

1	[170 g] pkg. favourite long-grain and wild rice mixture
2	large shallots, chopped
8	broccoli florets, cut into 2" [5 cm] lengths
4	thick sole fillets
8	sheets phyllo pastry
1/4	cup [60 mL] melted butter
	Lemon pepper
	Grated peel and juice of 1 lemon

1. Cook the rice mixture according to package directions, sautéing the chopped shallots in the butter in the initial step. Cool.

2. Steam, microwave or boil broccoli florets until about half-way cooked. Drain, rinse in cold water, drain again.

3. Place sole fillets flat on counter, underside up. Place 2 broccoli pieces on each piece of fish, with the stems towards the middle and the flower ends facing out. Roll each into a fat roll. Set aside.

4. Preheat oven to 425°F [220°C]. Place 1 sheet of phyllo pastry flat on counter with the long side facing you; brush quickly with some melted butter. Place a second sheet on top and repeat the butter.

5. Place about 3/4 cup [175 mL] rice mixture in the centre of the long side, about 1-1/2" [3.75 cm] away from the edge nearest you. Sprinkle with lemon pepper. Top with a sole roll, sprinkle generously with lemon peel and juice. Fold the 1-1/2" [3.75 cm] border nearest you up towards the sole; fold in the two sides; roll away from you, holding sides in on top of sole. You should have a fully encased package with sides folded in.

6. Brush each roll with melted butter. Bake about 15-17 minutes, depending on thickness of the sole. Phyllo should look browned and flaky. This complete meal in one roll only needs a salad or a steamed vegetable accompaniment.

Calories: 602;
Protein 24 g;
Carbohydrate 59 g;
Fibre 4.1 g;
Fat 30 g/serving

tomato prawn pizza

MAKES 4 SERVINGS

1	large thin-shell pizza crust
	Cornmeal [optional]
1/2	cup [125 mL] deli salsa, drained*
1/2	lb. [250 g] raw prawn tails, deveined**
1/2	small red onion, thinly sliced into rings
1	[1/2 oz./14 g] pkg. fresh oregano, chopped
1	ripe tomato, thinly sliced
	Black pepper
2	oz. [60 g] shaved or grated Parmesan or Asiago cheese

*We purchased a tub of Que Pasa salsa, but choose any favourite brand.
**If the prawn tails are frozen when you buy them, simply place them in a bowl of cold water while you prepare the remaining ingredients. They will be thawed enough to shell and devein in several minutes.

Calories: 458;
Protein 29 g;
Carbohydrate 63 g;
Fibre 1.5 g;
Fat 10 g/serving

1. Preheat the oven to 450°F [230°C].

2. Place the pizza crust on a cookie sheet that has been sprinkled with cornmeal [if using]. Spread with the drained salsa, leaving an uncovered rim around the edge.

3. Spread the dried and shelled prawn tails evenly over the salsa; cover with onion rings, oregano and slices of tomato.

4. Shake a good amount of black pepper over top.

5. Bake for about 5 minutes.

6. Sprinkle cheese over pizza; return to oven for another 4-5 minutes until the prawns have just turned pink and the crust is browned. Serve at once.

snapper veracruz

MAKES 4 SERVINGS

2	Tbsp. [30 mL] vegetable oil
4	red snapper boneless fillets [about 4-5 oz./120-150g each]
1	cup [250 mL] chopped onion
3	garlic cloves, minced
1	[28 fl. oz./796 mL] tin Italian plum tomatoes, chopped
1/2	tsp. [3 mL] salt
1/2	tsp. [3 mL] black pepper
3	Tbsp. [45 mL] fresh lime juice
2	tsp. [10 mL] chili powder
1/4	cup [60 mL] chopped cilantro
1/3	cup [75 mL] pimento-stuffed green olives

1. Heat oil in large skillet until bubbly; add snapper fillets, sautéing on both sides for about 1-2 minutes until browned but not fully cooked. Remove; keep warm.

2. Add onion and garlic to pan, sautéing until onion is nearly soft.

3. Add remaining ingredients except cilantro and olives; simmer, stirring occasionally, about 15 minutes to thicken.

4. Add cilantro, olives and snapper fillets. Mix gently to coat fillets in sauce. Simmer another 1-2 minutes. Serve at once.

*Calories: 274;
Protein 27 g;
Carbohydrate 19 g;
Fibre 2.4 g;
Fat 10 g/serving*

barbecued salmon with lemon, capers and orzo

MAKES 4 SERVINGS

1-1/4	lb. [0.5 kg] boneless salmon fillet
2/3	cup [150 mL] chopped fresh parsley
	Grated peel and juice of 2 large lemons
6	garlic cloves, minced
1/4	cup [60 mL] drained capers, divided
1/4	cup [60 mL] Balsamic vinegar
6	Tbsp. [90 mL] extra-virgin olive oil
1-1/4	cups [310 mL] orzo*

Orzo is a rice-shaped pasta, available in the dried pasta section.

Calories: 406;
Protein 30 g;
Carbohydrate 29 g;
Fibre 0.4 g;
Fat 19 g/serving

1. Cut salmon into serving-size portions; place in bowl.

2. Combine parsley, lemon peel and juice, garlic and half the capers in a food processor or in a bowl with a hand-held blender. Add vinegar and olive oil; process until well mixed but still rough-textured. Pour 3 Tbsp. [45 mL] of mixture over the salmon pieces; mix with your hands until all salmon is coated. Cover with plastic wrap; refrigerate overnight.

3. Cover and refrigerate remaining dressing.

4. Remove reserved dressing from refrigerator; stir in remaining whole capers.

5. Cook orzo in salted boiling water, about 12 minutes or until tender but not mushy. Drain well; rinse in hot water; drain well again.

6. While orzo is cooking, preheat barbecue to medium-high heat; barbecue salmon pieces, skin-side down, brushing with any remaining marinade as you cook. When salmon is done and orzo is cooked, toss hot orzo with reserved dressing [not the left-over salmon marinade].

7. Divide among 4 dinner plates and top each mound of orzo with a piece of barbecued salmon.

Serving suggestion: This dish is perfect with a crisp green salad on the side.

parmesan crusted halibut with rösti potatoes

MAKES 4 SERVINGS

Rösti Potatoes:
4	slices bacon, chopped
2	Tbsp. [30 mL] diced onion
4	medium Yukon Gold potatoes
1/4	cup [60 mL] unsalted butter, divided
	Salt and freshly ground black pepper

Fish:
1/2	cup [125 mL] coarse fresh bread crumbs
1/2	cup [125 mL] freshly grated Parmesan cheese
	Freshly ground black pepper
1	egg, beaten
1	lb. [500 g] fresh halibut fillets, about 4 fillets, 3/4" [2 cm] thick
	Light sour cream
	Freshly squeezed lemon juice

Calories: 668; Protein 47 g; Carbohydrate 56 g; Fibre 4.1 g; Fat 28 g/serving

1. Sauté bacon in a 6" [15 cm] skillet for about 5 minutes. Add onion and sauté until soft, about 2 minutes. Drain off fat; remove bacon and onions to a paper towel-lined plate and set aside.

2. Peel potatoes and grate coarsely. You should have about 4 cups [1 L] lightly packed grated potatoes. Using your hands or a piece of cheesecloth, squeeze out as much moisture as possible.

3. Melt 1 Tbsp. [15 mL] butter in a 6" [15 cm] skillet. Distribute 1/4 of the grated potatoes evenly over the bottom of the pan. Scatter 1/4 of the bacon-onion mixture evenly over top. Sprinkle with salt and pepper. Press down with a spatula and fry over medium heat for 5 minutes until golden or crispy on the bottom. Invert rösti onto a plate and slide back into the pan to cook the other side. Fry for another 5 minutes, shaking pan to prevent sticking, and transfer rösti to a parchment-lined baking sheet. Repeat process until you have 4 röstis on a baking sheet. Set aside, uncovered.

4. Preheat oven to 400°F [200°C].

5. Combine bread crumbs, Parmesan and pepper in a bowl. Stir to blend.

6. Dip halibut into egg and roll in bread crumb mixture. Place fish on a parchment-lined baking sheet. Bake in the centre of oven for 10 minutes per 1" [2.5 cm] of thickness or until fish is opaque and flakes easily with a fork. Be careful not to overbake.

7. About 5 minutes before the halibut is done, warm röstis by placing the baking tray of röstis, uncovered, on the rack in the oven below the halibut. For extra-crispy röstis, place in the oven at the same time as the halibut. To serve, remove röstis to heated serving dishes. Top each rösti with halibut and serve with sour cream and lemon juice.

seafood stuffed portobellos

MAKES 4 TO 6 SERVINGS

14	"Mini Portobello" mushrooms
1	[250 mL] bottle No Fat Italian Dressing
1/2	lb. [250 g] crab, shrimp, imitation crab and/or other seafood
1	[250 g] tub light Smoked Salmon Cream Cheese
1/2	bunch green onions, minced
1	roasted red bell pepper, minced*
	Grated peel and juice of 1 large lemon
2	tsp. [10 mL] puréed Garlic & Jalapeño**
1	[1/2 oz./14 g] pkg. fresh oregano, minced
1/4	cup [60 mL] fine dry bread crumbs
1/3-1/2	cup [75-125 mL] shredded Emmenthal cheese
	Salt and black pepper, to taste

*Slice peppers in half, remove seeds and place, cut side down, on a baking sheet. Broil until blackened. Cover until cool, then pull off skins. Also available prepared in some deli departments.
**Available in the produce department in small jars. If unavailable substitute a combination of 1-1/2 tsp. [8 mL] puréed garlic and 1/2 tsp. [3 mL] minced Jalapeño pepper [adjust the amount of Jalapeño depending on your taste].

Calories: 292;
Protein 19 g;
Carbohydrate 18.8 g;
Fibre 2.3 g;
Fat 16.2 g/serving

1. Remove and discard mushroom stems and brush to clean. Place in a bowl with the Italian dressing. Toss well to coat. Let stand while preparing the filling. [Mushrooms can marinate up to 4 hours before filling.]

2. Combine all other ingredients except the Emmenthal cheese. Mix well.

3. Place mushroom caps in a single layer in a shallow baker, leaving a little marinade in each cap. Discard remaining marinade.

4. Top all mushroom caps with filling. Spread Emmenthal cheese on top.

5. Preheat oven to 350°F [180°C]. Bake mushrooms about 20 minutes or until cheese has melted and tops are browning. Place under the broiler for the last couple of minutes to fully brown the tops, if desired.

seafood
stuffed
portobellos

wok fried
crab with
ginger and
black beans

wok fried crab with ginger and black beans

MAKES 2 SERVINGS

1	live Dungeness crab, about 2 lbs. [1 kg]
2	Tbsp. [30 mL] peanut or canola oil

Sauce:

1	Tbsp. [15 mL] peanut or canola oil
2	Tbsp. [30 mL] finely chopped peeled ginger root
1	Tbsp. [15 mL] minced garlic
1	Tbsp. [15 mL] minced shallot
1/2	cup [125 mL] water
1	Tbsp. + 2 tsp. [25 mL] rice wine vinegar
1	Tbsp. + 2 tsp. [25 mL] soy sauce
2	tsp. [10 mL] Chinese chili paste or Sambal Oelek*
1	Tbsp. [15 mL] fermented black beans, lightly rinsed
2	tsp. [10 mL] cornstarch dissolved in 1 Tbsp. [15 mL] cold water

*A hot Indonesian pepper paste found in small jars in the ethnic foods section.

---

1. To make the sauce: Heat oil in a small saucepan over medium-high heat. Add the ginger, garlic and shallots; sauté about 2 minutes or until softened.

2. Add the water, vinegar, soy sauce, chili paste and black beans; bring to a simmer. Cook the sauce 5 minutes, stirring.

3. Add the dissolved cornstarch and simmer, stirring frequently, until the sauce thickens and becomes glossy, about 2 more minutes.

4. Remove from the heat and set aside.

5. To clean the crab: Pull off the top shell, discard the grey gills and rinse the crab thoroughly. Pull off the claws and legs and chop the body in half. Rinse the crab thoroughly and set aside.

6. Heat a wok over high heat; add the oil and toss in the crab pieces. Stir-fry the crab about 3 minutes.

7. Add 1/4 cup [60 mL] water and cover the pan with a lid. Steam the crab 2 minutes, then remove the lid and add the sauce. Cook the crab, uncovered, stirring constantly, about 3-4 minutes or until the sauce thickens and coats the crab.

8. Transfer the crab to a platter and pour any remaining sauce over top.
Serve immediately.

Calories: 611;
Protein 80 g;
Carbohydrate 12 g;
Fibre 0.3 g;
Fat 25 g/serving

grilled bass with roasted garlic citrus baste

MAKES 4 SERVINGS

1	Tbsp. [15 mL] extra-virgin olive oil
6	large garlic cloves, peeled
	Grated peel and juice of 1 large lemon
	Juice of 1 large orange
	Juice of 1 large lime
4	[4 oz./125 g] bass fillets*
1	large baking potato
1	medium onion, thinly sliced
1-1/2	Tbsp. [25 mL] minced fresh thyme
	Salt and black pepper

Snapper, cod or halibut fillets all work well in this recipe.

Calories: 245;
Protein 28 g;
Carbohydrate 13 g;
Fibre 2.6 g;
Fat 8.8 g/serving

1. Heat oil in large oven-proof skillet. Add garlic cloves; toss until browned and soft. Remove and mash. Add to peel and juices, mixing well to combine.

2. Place pieces of bass in a large bowl, pouring the citrus-garlic mixture over top. Let stand 1/2 hour.

3. Over medium heat, reheat the oil remaining in skillet, pouring in some of the citrus marinade.

4. Shred the peeled potato using a food processor or a grater; place in colander over the sink and rinse thoroughly with cold water to remove the starch. Dry very well on paper towel. [Use the shredded potato quickly as it will turn brown if it sits in the colander for very long.] Add to skillet along with the onion. Turn heat to low and cook, turning occasionally, until both onion and potato are nearly cooked.

5. Add a generous amount of salt and pepper and the thyme, along with some more of the citrus marinade, mixing well to combine.

6. Preheat broiler. Place bass pieces upside down on top of the onion and potato mixture. Drizzle some of the citrus marinade over the fish. Place pan under the broiler. Broil about 4-5 minutes.

7. Turn fish, drizzling the last of the marinade over top. Replace under broiler for another 4-5 minutes or until fish is cooked through and starting to brown on top. [Usually fish takes about 10 minutes per 1"/2.5 cm of thickness.]

8. Serve at once on heated plates with fresh asparagus and crusty bread or flatbread.

chilled salmon with watercress sauce
MAKES 4 SERVINGS

Salmon:

2	cups [500 mL] dry white wine
4	cups [1 L] water
1	cooking onion, sliced
2	lemons, sliced
1	cup [250 mL] chopped celery
4	generous sprigs parsley
1	tsp. [5 mL] coarse salt
1/2	tsp. [3 mL] whole black peppercorns
4	skinless, boneless salmon fillets [6 oz./180 g each]

Watercress Sauce:

1	bunch watercress, washed and dried
	Finely grated peel of 1 lemon
1	garlic clove, coarsely chopped
1	Tbsp. [15 mL] finely minced fresh chives
1/2	cup [125 mL] light mayonnaise
1/2	cup [125 mL] plain low-fat yogurt
2	tsp. [10 mL] freshly squeezed lemon juice
1/4	tsp. [1 mL] coarse salt
2	each yellow and red vine-ripened tomatoes, quartered
2	tsp. [10 mL] capers, rinsed and drained
	Butter lettuce

1. Place first 8 ingredients in a pot large enough to hold salmon in a single layer. Bring to a boil. Cover and simmer for 30 minutes.

2. Strain and return broth to pan. Immerse salmon in liquid making sure fish is covered. Add a little water if needed. Bring to a boil and reduce heat to simmer for 10 minutes per 1" [2.5 cm] of thickness. Do not overcook; fish is done when flesh is opaque in the centre. Using a slotted spoon, remove fillets and place on a platter to cool.

3. Cover and refrigerate until ready to serve.

4. To make sauce, coarsely chop the entire bunch of watercress leaves and stems and place in a blender or food processor.

5. Add lemon peel, garlic and chives and whirl until coarsely chopped.

6. Add mayonnaise and yogurt and process until watercress is very finely chopped.

7. Add lemon juice and salt and pulse to blend. Transfer sauce to a serving bowl.

8. To serve, line 4 plates with butter lettuce leaves. Arrange chilled salmon on top with 4 wedges of yellow and red tomato. Garnish with Watercress Sauce and capers.

Calories: 422;
Protein 39 g;
Carbohydrate 19 g;
Fibre 5.1 g;
Fat 18 g/serving

[101]

halibut in white wine with rosemary

MAKES 6 SERVINGS

2	lbs. [1 kg]	boned and skinned halibut fillets, about 3/4" [1.75 cm] thick
1/3	cup [75 mL]	all-purpose flour
1/4	tsp. [1 mL]	salt
5	Tbsp. [75 mL]	olive oil, divided
1		large onion, finely diced
1		large carrot, finely diced
3/4	cup [175 mL]	white wine or chicken broth
1	Tbsp. [15 mL]	minced fresh parsley
2	tsp. [10 mL]	finely minced fresh rosemary or 1/2 tsp. [2 mL] dried rosemary
		Freshly ground black pepper

Calories 339;
Protein 35.8 g;
Carbohydrate 8 g;
Fibre 1 g;
Fat 15.3 g/serving

1. Wash halibut fillets in cold water and pat dry.

2. Combine flour, salt and pepper in a large bowl. Stir to blend. Dredge fillets in seasoned flour and set aside.

3. Heat 3 Tbsp. [45 mL] oil in a large skillet. Sauté several pieces of fish in a single layer over medium heat for 5 minutes. Then turn and continue to sauté another 3-4 minutes. Remove to a warm platter and keep warm.

4. Repeat with remaining fillets, adding a little more oil if necessary.

5. Meanwhile, in a skillet pour remaining 2 Tbsp. [30 mL] oil. Add finely diced onion and carrot; sauté over medium heat until onion is soft and translucent, about 5 minutes. Stir often.

6. Add wine, parsley and rosemary and bring to a boil. Boil vigorously until reduced by half, about 2 minutes. Drizzle sauce over halibut fillets and serve immediately.

classic prawn newburg

MAKES 4 SERVINGS

24	large tiger prawns [with shell]
1	cup [250 mL] clam nectar or fish stock
1	cup [250 mL] half and half cream
4	sprigs fresh rosemary
2	Tbsp. [30 mL] unsalted butter
3	small shallots, minced
1/3	lb. [150 g] button mushrooms, sliced
3	Tbsp. [45 mL] all-purpose flour
1/4	tsp. [2 mL] salt
1/4	tsp. [2 mL] white pepper
1/4	tsp. [2 mL] ground nutmeg
5	Tbsp. [75 mL] dry sherry
1	egg
1	Tbsp. [15 mL] half and half cream
1/4	cup [60 mL] minced fresh parsley

1. Bring a pot of salted water to a boil and add prawns. Cook about 2 minutes; remove and rinse in cold water. Peel, devein and set aside.

2. Combine clam nectar, cream and rosemary in a glass measure; microwave on high [100%] power until very hot but not boiling [about 3 minutes].

3. Meanwhile, melt butter in a medium saucepan; when hot, add shallots and mushrooms. Stir and cook 3-4 minutes or until shallots are softened.

4. Stir in flour and cook another minute.

5. Gradually stir in the hot liquid [including the rosemary sprigs]; stir and cook until you have a smooth, thickened sauce. Stir in the salt, pepper, nutmeg and sherry.

6. Use a fork to beat the egg together with the 1 Tbsp. [15 mL] cream. Stir a little of the hot sauce into this and when totally combined, stir the whole mixture into the sauce in the pan. Continue cooking and stirring over low heat until the sauce thickens a little more.

7. Add the prawns and remove the rosemary.

8. Serve over rice or noodles; top with parsley.

Calories: 217;
Protein 14 g;
Carbohydrate 10 g;
Fibre 1.5 g;
Fat 12 g/serving

herbed seafood stew

MAKES 4 SERVINGS

1	Tbsp. [15 mL] olive oil
1	large onion, sliced
1	small fennel bulb, thinly sliced
2	garlic cloves, minced
1	celery stalk, sliced
1	[28 fl. oz./796 mL] tin diced tomatoes
1	[187 mL] bottle dry white wine*
3	Tbsp. [45 mL] tomato paste
1	Tbsp. [15 mL] Worcestershire sauce
1/4	tsp. [1 mL] cayenne
4	tsp. [20 mL] minced fresh thyme
4	tsp. [20 mL] minced fresh oregano
1/2	tsp. [3 mL] salt
1/2	tsp. [3 mL] coarse black pepper
12	large mussels, well scrubbed
1/2	lb. [250 g] solid white fish [bass, halibut, snapper, cod], cut into chunks
	Chopped fresh parsley

Unsweetened white grape juice or clam nectar can be substituted.

Calories: 217;
Protein 17 g;
Carbohydrate 23 g;
Fibre 4.9 g;
Fat 6 g/serving

1. Heat oil in large Dutch oven until hot. Over medium heat, add onion, fennel, garlic and celery. Cook until just tender, stirring occasionally.

2. Add the tomatoes, wine [or juice], tomato paste, Worcestershire, cayenne, herbs, salt and pepper. Mix well. Bring to the boil and cook about 5 to 6 minutes.

3. Add mussels and chunks of fish; cover tightly and cook over low to medium heat about 7-8 minutes. Check to see if mussels have opened. Discard any unopened ones.

4. Serve at once in large shallow bowls.

fiery prawn wok

MAKES 4 SERVINGS

2	tsp. [10 mL] whole black peppercorns
1	tsp. [5 mL] whole coriander seeds
4	garlic cloves, minced
1	[1-1/2"/3.75 cm] piece fresh ginger, peeled, grated
1-2	tsp. [5-10 mL] crushed red pepper flakes
1/2	tsp. [3 mL] salt
2	Tbsp. [30 mL] liquid honey
1-2	tsp. [5-10 mL] Sambal Oelek*
3	Tbsp. [45 mL] dry sherry
24	large prawns, peeled, deveined
1	large red bell pepper, seeded, chunked
1/2	cup [125 mL] honey roasted peanuts
1	bunch green onions, trimmed, each cut into 4 pieces
	Chopped cilantro [optional]

*A hot Indonesian pepper paste found in small jars in the ethnic foods section.

1. Place peppercorns and coriander seeds in a small skillet and dry-fry them over medium heat, shaking pan occasionally, until they start to pop and give off an aroma.
2. Remove from heat and combine with the following 7 ingredients in a blender, food processor or bowl with a handheld blender. Process until a paste is formed.
3. Combine paste and prawns in a bowl and mix well to coat all prawns. Cover and refrigerate overnight or at least 4-6 hours.
4. Heat a wok or skillet to high; add prawns and paste mixture. Stir-fry about 1-2 minutes or until prawns are about half cooked [still translucent but turning pink].
5. Add bell pepper and peanuts to pan and cook another minute.
6. Add green onions and cilantro [if using]; toss for 30 seconds and serve at once on hot plates with rice or noodles.

Calories: 213;
Protein 14 g;
Carbohydrate 16 g;
Fibre 3.4 g;
Fat 10 g/serving

[105]

PHOTO: JOHN SHERLOCK

tuna souvlakia

MAKES 8 SERVINGS

2	lbs. [1 kg] fresh yellowfin tuna fillets
2	Tbsp. [30 mL] olive oil
	Juice of 1 large lemon
1	Tbsp. [15 mL] dried marjoram
1	tsp. [5 mL] Dijon mustard
	Salt and freshly ground black pepper
8	metal skewers
1	red onion, peeled and quartered
2	green bell peppers, seeded and cut into chunks
8	pitted black olives
1	[250 mL] container tzatziki sauce*

*Avaiable in the deli section.

Calories: 209;
Protein 31 g;
Carbohydrate 6 g;
Fibre 1.4 g;
Fat 6 g/serving

1. Cut fillets into 1" [2.5 cm] chunks.

2. Whisk together olive oil, lemon juice, marjoram, mustard, and salt and pepper to taste. Pour marinade over cubes of tuna and toss together to evenly coat. Refrigerate for 1 hour.

3. When ready to cook, take onion layers apart. Reserving the fish marinade, thread tuna cubes onto metal skewers alternating with pieces of onion and green pepper. Finish each skewer with a black olive.

4. Preheat barbecue to medium-high and place skewers on greased grill. Close lid and cook, turning once, for about 5 minutes or until fish is opaque and flakes easily with a fork. Tuna should still be a little pink in the centre. [If overcooked it becomes papery.]

5. Brush occasionally with marinade while grilling. Discard remaining marinade.

6. Serve skewers with dollops of tzatziki, lots of fresh bread and a salad.

steamed mussels and clams
with coconut milk and lemon grass

MAKES 4 SERVINGS

1	[1-1/2"/4 cm] piece of fresh ginger, peeled
4	garlic cloves, peeled
3/4	cup [175 mL] water, divided
1	Tbsp. [15 mL] olive oil
1	medium red onion, peeled, finely chopped
2	Jalapeño peppers, halved, seeded, finely chopped
2	stalks lemon grass, inner white bulb only, thinly sliced crosswise
2	tsp. [10 mL] ground cumin
1	tsp. [5 mL] ground coriander
1/2	tsp. [3 mL] turmeric
1-1/2	cups [375 mL] unsweetened coconut milk [not cream]
	Salt and freshly ground black pepper to taste
1-1/2	lbs. [750 g] mussels, scrubbed, beards removed
1-1/2	lbs. [750 g] clams, scrubbed
2	Tbsp. [30 mL] fresh lime juice
	Lime wedges, for serving

---

1. Coarsely chop the ginger and garlic in a food processor. Add 1/2 cup [125 mL] water and process until almost smooth; set aside.

2. Heat the oil in a heavy saucepan large and deep enough to hold all of the shellfish. Add the onion; cover and cook over low heat, stirring occasionally, until softened, about 10 minutes.

3. Add the Jalapeños, lemon grass, cumin, coriander, turmeric and the garlic and ginger purée. Cook mixture over medium heat, stirring, about 3 minutes or until most of the liquid has evaporated.

4. Stir in coconut milk, the remaining water and salt and pepper to taste. Bring to a simmer. Remove from the heat.

5. At this point the sauce can be stored at room temperature, well covered, up to 4 hours.

6. When ready to cook the shellfish, bring the coconut broth to a boil. Stir in the mussels and clams. Cover and cook over medium heat just until the mussels and clams open, about 5-7 minutes; discard any shellfish that don't open.

7. Stir in the lime juice and adjust seasonings with additional salt and pepper.

8. Spoon the mussels, clams and their broth into shallow bowls. Serve immediately with lime wedges.

Calories: 367;
Protein 48 g;
Carbohydrate 20 g;
Fibre 1.1 g;
Fat 10 g/serving

[meatless meals]

Four-Cheese Avocado Quesadillas
Black Bean Chili
Grilled Vegetable Pizza
Mixed Vegetable Curry
Tofu with Ginger and Spinach
Traditional Vegetable Stir-fry with Sesame and Garlic
Eggplant Rolls with Florentine Filling in Marinara Sauce
Spring Veggie Clafouti
Instant Hot Pepper Pot
Leek and Portobello Pizza
Italian Mushroom Orzo
Vegetarian Chili and Cheese Casserole
Cornbread Squares with Mushroom Ragout
Spanakopita Triangles

PHOTO: ROSS DURANT

four-cheese avocado quesadillas

MAKES 4 SERVINGS

4	[9"/23 cm] flour tortillas
6	Tbsp. [90 mL] chopped sun-dried tomatoes, reserving oil
1	[4.5 fl. oz./125 mL] tin sliced black olives
1	ripe avocado, thinly sliced
2	cups [500 mL] mixed grated 4-cheese mixture*
1	Tbsp. [15 mL] oil from sun-dried tomatoes
	No-fat sour cream [optional]
	Chopped green onions [optional]
	Hot salsa [optional]

We used a grated mixture found in plastic packages in the dairy section.

Calories: 533;
Protein 21 g;
Carbohydrate 29 g;
Fibre 5.6 g;
Fat 37 g/serving

1. Prepare all ingredients as described above before starting preparation.
2. You will need a large [preferably non-stick] skillet. Lay tortillas on counter. On one half of each place 1/4 of the following: sun-dried tomatoes, black olives, avocado slices and 4-cheese mixture.
3. Fold the empty half of each tortilla over top of the filling; press slightly.
4. Heat tomato oil in skillet over medium heat; add 2 folded and filled tortillas, placing them cheese side down.
5. After a couple of minutes, use two wide lifters to turn them over; cook other side. Both sides should be golden brown with the cheese melting inside. Repeat with remaining 2 filled tortillas.
6. Cut each quesadilla into four triangles and serve on a heated platter, accompanying them with the optional toppings listed above. Your guests can help themselves to each topping as desired.

PHOTO: JOHN SINAL

black bean chili

MAKES 4 TO 6 SERVINGS

1	Tbsp. [15 mL] vegetable oil
1	medium onion, diced
3	garlic cloves, minced
1	green bell pepper, seeded, diced
2	celery stalks with leaves, diced
1	[28 fl. oz./796 mL] tin diced tomatoes, undrained
3	Tbsp. [45 mL] minced chipotle peppers [in adobo sauce]*
1	Tbsp. [5 mL] chili powder
1	tsp. [5 mL] dried oregano leaves, crushed
1	tsp. [5 mL] granulated sugar
1/2	tsp. [3 mL] salt
1/4	tsp. [2 mL] freshly ground black pepper
1-1/4	cup [310 mL] frozen corn niblets
2	[19 fl. oz./540 mL] tins black beans, drained, rinsed
1/4	cup [60 mL] minced fresh cilantro
	Grated light "old" Cheddar cheese [optional]
	No-fat sour cream [optional]

*Found in tins in the Mexican foods section.

---

1. Heat oil in a large Dutch oven. When hot, add onion, garlic, green pepper and celery.
2. Stir and sauté until onion softens. Add all remaning ingredients except beans and cilantro.
3. Stir and simmer with lid tilted for 40 minutes. Add rinsed black beans and cilantro. Heat 10-15 minutes.

Serving suggestion: Serve in warm bowls topped with the grated cheese or no-fat sour cream if desired.

Calories: 400;
Protein: 22.6 g;
Carbohydrate 71.8 g;
Fibre 13 g;
Fat 4.6 g/serving

grilled vegetable pizza
MAKES ONE 12" [30 CM] PIZZA

1	medium eggplant, cut into 1/2" [1.25 cm] slices
1	medium zucchini, cut lengthwise into 1/2" [1.25 cm] slices
1	large red onion, cut into 1/2" ([1.25 cm] slices, secured with toothpick
2	sweet red bell peppers, cored, seeded, quartered
1/2	lb. [250 g] large mushrooms, wiped, trimmed
2	Tbsp. [30 mL] olive oil
	Grated peel of 1 lemon
1-2	garlic cloves, minced
1	tsp. [5 mL] each Mrs. Dash Seasoning and dried oregano
1	[12"/30 cm] pizza shell [home-made or purchased]
1	cup [250 mL] tomato sauce
1	cup [250 mL] crumbled Feta cheese
	Salt and freshly ground pepper, to taste
	Fresh oregano leaves
	Pitted Greek olives
	Cornmeal

Calories: 332;
Protein 10 g;
Carbohydrate 46 g;
Fibre 3.6 g;
Fat 12 g/slice

1. In a large bowl, toss together first 9 ingredients. Cover with plastic wrap; marinate in refrigerator while barbecue heats. Lightly oil or spray grill.
2. Place marinated vegetable slices on grill; barbecue until tender and slightly charred [8-15 minutes].
3. Remove vegetables from grill; let cool; cut into 1/2" [1.25 cm] strips; set aside.
4. Preheat oven to 475°F [240°C]. Place pizza shell on a baking sheet sprinkled with cornmeal. Spread sauce over shell; arrange grilled vegetables on top; sprinkle with Feta cheese; season generously with salt and freshly ground pepper, to taste.
5. Bake on bottom rack – 18-20 minutes for fresh dough; 12-16 minutes for pre-baked shells. Garnish with fresh oregano leaves and olives before slicing and serving.

Note: Vegetables can be broiled instead of barbecued.

mixed vegetable curry

MAKES 4 SERVINGS

6	small, waxy potatoes, halved
1/2	cup [125 mL] chopped green beans, cut into 1" [2.5 cm] pieces
1/2	cup [125 mL] cauliflower florets
1/2	cup [125 mL] broccoli florets
1/2	cup [125 mL] chopped carrots, cut into 1" [2.5 cm] pieces
1/2	cup [125 mL] frozen peas
1/2	red bell pepper, seeded, cut into 1" [2.5 cm] chunks
1/2	cup [125 mL] frozen corn
1/2	cup [125 mL] button mushrooms
2	Tbsp. [30 mL] vegetable oil
1	tsp. [5 mL] cumin seed
1/2	tsp. [3 mL] mustard seed
1	tsp. [5 mL] ground turmeric
1	Tbsp. [15 mL] minced fresh ginger
3	garlic cloves, minced
1	whole dried red chili pepper
1	tsp. [5 mL] granulated sugar
1	cup [250 mL] low-fat yogurt [optional]
1-1/2	tsp. [8 mL] cornstarch [optional]
	Salt, to taste

1. Boil the potatoes until tender; drain.

2. Blanch the remaining vegetables separately in boiling water until almost tender [they should stay crunchy]. Drain well.

3. Heat oil in a large skillet; sauté the spices gently until the garlic is golden brown and the chile is nearly burnt. Reduce heat. Stir in the drained vegetables; add salt and sugar. [If you want a creamier consistency, gradually add the yogurt mixed with the cornstarch.] Toss the vegetables to coat with spices.

4. Reduce heat to low and cook, covered, for 5 minutes or until hot.

Calories: 277;
Protein 9.4 g;
Carbohydrate 46 g;
Fibre 6.7 g;
Fat 7.8 g/serving

PHOTO: ROBERT KENNEY

tofu with ginger and spinach

MAKES 3 TO 4 SERVINGS

1	[375 g] pkg. firm tofu
2	large Portobello mushrooms
3	Tbsp. [45 mL] black bean sauce*
5	Tbsp. [75 mL] dry white wine, divided
3	garlic cloves, minced
1-1/2	Tbsp. [25 mL] grated fresh ginger
1/2	tsp. [3 mL] crushed red pepper flakes
1	Tbsp. [15 mL] cornstarch
1	large green bell pepper
2	Tbsp. [30 mL] vegetable oil
1	[283 g] pkg. spinach, washed and trimmed

Use the liquid type of black bean sauce for a lighter taste or the thicker paste variety for a stronger taste.

Calories: 253;
Protein 18 g;
Carbohydrate 13 g;
Fibre 3.2 g;
Fat 15 g/serving

1. Cut the tofu into small cubes and set aside. Wipe the mushrooms and dice into similar-size cubes; set aside.

2. Mix together the next 5 ingredients, using only 3 Tbsp. [45 mL] of the wine. Set aside.

3. Combine the remaining 2 Tbsp. [30 mL] of wine with the cornstarch and set aside.

4. Seed and julienne the green bell pepper; set aside.

5. Heat the oil in a large wok to about 350°F [180°C]. Add the tofu and mushrooms; stir-fry about 1 minute. Add the black bean sauce mixture to the wok; stir-fry another 30 seconds. Stir in the cornstarch mixture. Add the bell pepper strips and spinach. Stir-fry about 1-2 minutes or until the sauce has thickened slightly and the spinach has wilted into the mixture.

Serving suggestion: Serve with brown rice or couscous.

traditional vegetable stir-fry with sesame and garlic

MAKES 4 ENTREE OR 6 SIDE DISH SERVINGS

2	large carrots
1	large onion
1	lb. [500 g] broccoli
1/4	lb. [125 g] snow peas
1	large green bell pepper
1	large red bell pepper
1/4	lb. [125 g] mushrooms
1/2	cup [125 mL] chicken broth with garlic and herbs
2	Tbsp. [30 mL] dark soy sauce
1/3	cup [75 mL] bottled chili sauce
2	Tbsp. [30 mL] HP Steak Sauce
2	Tbsp. [30 mL] packed brown sugar
4	tsp. [20 mL] sesame oil
1	Tbsp. [15 mL] cornstarch
1	Tbsp. [15 mL] vegetable oil
1/2	cup [125 mL] baking cashews [unsalted]*

*Available in the bulk food department.

1. Prepare all the vegetables before starting to cook: peel and cut carrots diagonally [making a 1/4 turn between each cut] to make pieces with maximum cut edges. Peel and chunk the onion. Break the broccoli into small florets. Trim the ends of the snow peas. Seed and chunk the green bell pepper. Seed and julienne the red bell pepper. Wipe and halve the mushrooms [quarter them if they are large].
2. Combine the next 7 ingredients; mix well.
3. Heat the oil in a large wok to about 375°F [190°C]. Add the carrots; stir-fry about 1-2 minutes. Add the onion; stir-fry 1 minute longer. Add the broccoli, snow peas, green and red pepper; stir-fry another 2 minutes. Add the mushrooms; stir-fry 30 seconds before adding the broth mixture. Stir-fry another 2 minutes, tossing to completely coat all pieces with the thickening sauce. Stir in the cashews. After 30 seconds, turn off the wok and serve with hot rice or noodles.

Calories: 338;
Protein 11 g;
Carbohydrate 41 g;
Fibre 8.7 g;
Fat 17 g/serving

eggplant rolls with florentine filling in a marinara sauce

MAKES 6 SERVINGS

2	large eggplants, about 1-1/4 lbs. [625 g] each*
	Cooking spray

Filling:

1	egg
1	Tbsp. [15 mL] finely minced fresh basil or 1/2 tsp. [3 mL] dried
1	tsp. [5 mL] minced fresh oregano or 1/4 tsp. [2 mL] dried
1/4	tsp. [2 mL] each salt and freshly ground black pepper
	Generous grating of fresh nutmeg
1/4	cup [60 mL] finely minced onion
1	garlic clove, finely minced
1-1/2	cups [375 mL] low-fat Quark cheese or drained Ricotta
1/4	cup [60 mL] freshly grated Parmigiano-Reggiano or Romano
4	oz. [120 g] fresh spinach, about 2 c. (500 mL)
1	[700 mL] jar commercially prepared basil and tomato sauce**
2	Tbsp. [30 mL] shredded Parmesan cheese
2	Tbsp. [30 mL] minced fresh flat parsley
	Finely grated peel of 1/2 lemon [optional]

*For a speedy alternative, use oven-ready cannelloni in place of eggplant and stuff shells with cheese and spinach filling. Add sauce and sufficient water as per package instructions before baking.
**If you prefer, substitute your favourite meatless pasta sauce.*

Calories: 201;
Protein 13.6 g;
Carbohydrate 23.5 g;
Fibre 7.6 g;
Fat 7.3 g/serving

1. Using a very sharp knife, thinly slice top and bottom off eggplants. Stand eggplant on cut bottom and thinly slice away the skin, rotating eggplant as you slice until all the skin is removed.
2. With each eggplant still standing on its cut end, slice eggplants into long, thin vertical slices about 1/2" [1.25 cm] thick.
3. Preheat oven to 400°F [200°C]. Lightly spray a large baking sheet with cooking spray.
4. Arrange eggplant slices in a single layer and bake 5 minutes. Flip and bake another 5 minutes. Do not worry if slices seem too firm; they will continue to soften as they cool.
5. To prepare filling, combine egg, herbs, seasonings, onion and garlic in a large bowl. Stir to blend. Add cheese and work in with a fork until blended. Wash and spin-dry spinach. Then stack leaves and slice crosswise into very thin strips. Fold into cheese mixture.
6. Place eggplant slices on work surface and with a thin palette knife or spatula gently spread each with equal amounts cheese and spinach filling.
7. Roll up jellyroll fashion and place seam-side down in a 9" x 13" [23 cm x 32.5 cm] casserole dish large enough to hold rolls in a single layer. Pour basil and tomato sauce evenly over top and spread out. Scatter shredded Parmesan over top. Loosely cover with foil and place in centre of the preheated oven. Bake 30 minutes or until sauce is bubbly and rolls are piping hot. [Alternatively, make ahead and refrigerate. Then bake same day for 45 minutes, or until sauce is bubbly and rolls are hot.]
8. Sprinkle with minced parsley and lemon peel if desired.

eggplant
rolls with
florentine
filling in a
marinara
sauce

spring
veggie
clafouti

spring veggie clafouti

MAKES 4 SERVINGS

4	Tbsp. [60 mL] vegetable oil
1	medium onion, chopped
1	cup [250 mL] all-purpose flour
3/4	tsp. [4 mL] salt
1/2	tsp. [3 mL] black pepper
3	eggs
1-1/2	cup [375 mL] 1% milk
2	Tbsp. [30 mL] minced mixed fresh herbs*
1	Tbsp. [15 mL] Dijon mustard
1	leek, cleaned, sliced
2	young bunch carrots, chopped
6	asparagus spears, trimmed, cut in 3/4" [2 cm] lengths
1/2	cup [125 mL] fresh English peas**
3	garlic cloves, minced
1/4	cup [60 mL] cold water

*In the test kitchen we used a mixture of sage, thyme and oregano.
**Frozen peas can be substituted (do not thaw).

1. Preheat oven to 475°F [240°C].
2. Combine oil and chopped onion, tossing together in an old 9" [23 cm] square thin metal cake pan. Place in the centre of oven and bake 10 minutes.
3. Meanwhile, beat or whisk together flour, salt, pepper, eggs, milk, herbs and mustard until smooth. Add vegetables and garlic and mix well.
4. Stir in the cold water at the end just before opening the oven door.
5. Pull the hot pan toward you and quickly pour the batter and vegetables into the hot oil and onions. Close the oven door quickly.
6. Bake about 35 minutes or until browned and slightly puffy [will not puff as much as Yorkshire pudding].
7. Cut into squares and serve at once as a side dish or brunch main course.

Calories: 410;
Protein 13.5 g;
Carbohydrate 48.2 g;
Fibre 4.9 g;
Fat 18.7 g/serving

instant hot pepper pot

MAKES 4 SERVINGS

1/4	cup [60 mL] olive oil
1	large onion, thinly sliced
2	large garlic cloves, minced
1	green bell pepper, seeded, chopped
1	red bell pepper, seeded, chopped
1	[19 fl. oz./540 mL] tin chickpeas [garbanzo beans], drained
1	[125 g] tin diced green chili peppers, drained
3	cups [750 mL] vegetable broth
2	Tbsp. [30 mL] tomato paste
	Crushed red pepper flakes
1/4	cup [60 mL] crumbled Feta cheese [optional]

Calories: 376;
Protein 13 g;
Carbohydrate 40 g;
Fibre 9. 1 g;
Fat 20 g/serving
(with cheese)

1. In a heavy-bottomed saucepan, heat oil over medium heat; cook onion for about 2 minutes or until soft.

2. Add garlic, green and red bell peppers and cook for 3-5 minutes or until peppers are slightly softened. Stir often.

3. Stir in chickpeas, chiles, broth and tomato paste and bring to a boil. Add red pepper flakes to taste.

4. Serve sprinkled with Feta cheese if desired.

leek and portobello pizza

MAKES 4 SERVINGS

3	Tbsp. [45 mL] vegetable oil
1	medium red onion, thinly sliced
3	leeks [pale part only], washed and thinly sliced
2	tsp. [10 mL] minced garlic
1-1/2 to 2	tsp. [7-10 mL] Sambal Oelek*
1	tsp. [5 mL] salt
1-1/2	tsp. [7 mL] coarse black pepper
2	large Portobello mushrooms, roughly chopped
1	[12"/30 cm] pizza crust
3/4	cup [175 mL] no-fat sour cream
	Shaved Parmesan cheese

*Sambal Oelek is an Indonesian hot pepper paste found in the ethnic foods section.
Available in both large and small jars.

1. Preheat oven to 400°F [200°C].
2. Heat oil in a large skillet. When hot, add onion, leeks, garlic, Sambal Oelek, salt and pepper. Sauté about 5 minutes over high heat until onions are soft and coloured. Leeks should still be brightly coloured. Remove from heat to a bowl.
3. Add Portobello mushrooms to pan and cook until slightly softened.
4. Place pizza crust on a baking sheet. Spread with sour cream. Spread onion mixture over top. Spread Portobellos over onion. Use a potato peeler to carve large shards of Parmesan and scatter over top of the pizza.
5. Bake 8-10 minutes or until hot and bubbly. Let sit 2 minutes before slicing.

Calories: 327;
Protein 7 g;
Carbohydrate 39 g;
Fibre 3.2 g;
Fat 17 g/serving

italian mushroom orzo

MAKES 6 SERVINGS

1	[14 g] pkg. dried mushrooms, such as chanterelles, oyster or mixed
2	Tbsp. [30 mL] butter
1	medium onion, diced
1	garlic clove, minced
1/2	[450 g] pkg. pearl barley, about 1 c. [250 mL]
8	oz. [250 g] fresh white mushrooms, sliced
1	[10 fl. oz. tin/284 mL] chicken broth
1/2-1	cup [125-250 mL] water
	Freshly ground black pepper
1	Tbsp. (15 mL) grated Parmesan cheese

Calories 206;
Protein 7.6 g;
Carbohydrate 33 g;
Fibre 7.5 g;
Fat 5.8 g/serving

1. Place dried mushrooms in a large bowl. Add enough water to cover. Set aside to soak for 20 minutes. Then drain and chop.

2. Meanwhile, melt butter in a large heavy-bottomed saucepan. Add onion and garlic; sauté over medium-low heat for about 5 minutes or until soft.

3. Turn heat to high and stir in barley. Continue to stir for 1 minute; add chopped dried and fresh mushrooms, chicken broth, 1 tin water plus 1/2 c. [125 mL] water; bring to a boil.

4. Cover, reduce heat to low and simmer for about 25 minutes or until barley is tender. Stir occasionally, adding a little more water if necessary. Stir in pepper to taste.

5. Sprinkle with Parmesan and serve.

vegeterian chili and cheese casserole

MAKES 4 TO 6 SERVINGS

2	Tbsp. [30 mL] vegetable oil
1	large onion, cut into wedges
3	garlic cloves, minced
1	cup [250 mL] raw long-grain white rice
1	[10 fl. oz./284 mL] tin Tomato Soup with Basil & Oregano
2-1/2	tins water
1 1/2	Tbsp. [25 mL] chili powder
1	tsp. [5 mL] salt
1	[125 mL] tin sliced Jalapeños, undrained
1	[1/2 oz./14 g] pkg. fresh oregano, minced
1 1/2	cups [375 mL] frozen lima beans
2	ripe tomatoes, seeded, cut into 8ths
1/2	bunch fresh spinach, washed, roughly chopped
3-1/2	oz. [100 g] "old" Cheddar cheese, cut in tiny dice
	No-fat sour cream (optional)

1. Preheat oven to 350°F [180°C]. Heat oil in large Dutch oven. When hot, add onion and garlic. Sauté 1-2 minutes until onion starts to soften.

2. Add rice and stir well to coat rice with oil. Gradually stir in soup and tins of water, chili powder, salt and jalapeños. Stir well and cover.

3. Place in oven for 40 minutes. At this point, stir well to distribute ingredients. Rice should be almost cooked. Add oregano and lima beans. Cover again and return to oven for another 20 minutes.

4. Add tomato wedges, spinach and diced cheese. Stir well, turn off oven and let covered casserole stand in oven with door open for 5 minutes. Stir to distribute melting cheese pieces and serve at once in warm bowls. Tomatoes, spinach and cheese should all still be visible and bright in colour – do not overheat at this stage.

5. Top each serving with no-fat sour cream if desired.

Calories: 398;
Protein 13.6 g;
Carbohydrate 56.2 g;
Fibre 5.7 g;
Fat 13.6 g/serving

cornbread squares with mushroom ragout

MAKES 6 SERVINGS

Cornbread:

2/3	cup [150 mL]	yellow cornmeal
1-1/3	cups [325 mL]	all-purpose flour
5	tsp. [25 mL]	baking powder
1	Tbsp. [15 mL]	granulated sugar
1	Tbsp. [15 mL]	chili powder
1	tsp. [5 mL]	chopped dried red chili peppers
1/4	tsp. [1 mL]	salt
1/2	cup [125 mL]	grated "old" Cheddar cheese
1		egg, beaten
1/4	cup [60 mL]	melted butter or margarine
1-1/3	cups [325 mL]	1% milk
3/4	cup [175 mL]	drained corn kernels*
1/4	cup [60 mL)	diced red or green bell pepper [optional]

Ragout:

2	Tbsp. [30 mL]	olive oil
1		medium onion, chopped
3		large garlic cloves, minced
3/4	lb. [375 g]	mixed fresh mushrooms, cut in large pieces**
1	[14 fl. oz/396 mL]	tin red kidney beans, drained
1/4	cup [60 mL]	brandy***
1	Tbsp. [15 mL]	Dijon mustard
1	[1/2 oz./14 g]	pkg. fresh thyme, chopped

*Corn can be frozen or canned.
**We used a mixture of Portobellos, button and crimini.
***Beef stock can be substituted.

Calories: 486;
Protein 15 g;
Carbohydrate 57 g;
Fibre 7.3 g;
Fat 20 g/serving

1. Preheat oven to 350°F [180°C]. Combine first 8 ingredients in a large bowl.

2. Combine next 5 ingredients in a small bowl and mix well. Add wet ingredients to dry; do not mix totally – just until moistened.

3. Turn batter into a sprayed [or lightly greased] 8" [20 cm] square cake pan. Bake about 35 minutes or until a toothpick inserted in the centre comes out clean.

4. Meanwhile, heat olive oil in a large skillet until hot. Add onion and garlic; cook 1 minute; add mushrooms and increase heat to high. Cook, stirring occasionally, until mushrooms regain their liquid.

5. Add the beans and the brandy mixed with mustard and thyme; cook and stir another 3-4 minutes or until liquid evaporates and leaves a thick mushroom ragout.

6. Cut the warm cornbread into squares and place on heated dinner plates.

7. Spoon ragout over and around cornbread.

spanakopita triangles

MAKES 24 TRIANGLES

1	[454 g] box frozen phyllo pastry dough*
2	tsp. [10 mL] olive oil
1	small onion, diced, about 1/2 cup [125 mL]
2	garlic cloves, minced
1	[300 g] pkg. frozen chopped spinach, thawed
1/4	cup [60 mL] chopped pitted Calamata olives
2	oz. [60 g] Feta cheese, rinsed, drained, crumbled [about 1/2 c./125mL]
3	Tbsp. [45 mL] grated Parmesan cheese
1	Tbsp. [15 mL] fresh lemon juice
1	tsp. [5 mL] dried oregano
1	egg, beaten
3/4	cup [175 mL] unsalted butter, melted or unseasoned olive oil cooking spray
1/3	cup [75 mL] unsalted butter, melted

*Phyllo [sometimes labelled filo] is usually sold frozen. It's best to thaw the dough in the refrigerator. Alternatively, you can thaw it at room temperature for 1 to 2 hours, providing your kitchen is not too warm.

1. Heat 2 tsp. [10 mL] oil in a medium saucepan; add onion and garlic. Sauté over medium heat until almost soft. Stir often. Remove to a large bowl. Squeeze excess moisture from spinach and add to onion, along with chopped olives, Feta, Parmesan and seasonings. Add pepper to taste. Stir in egg. Set aside.

2. Remove phyllo from package. Gently unroll the sheets and place flat on a kitchen towel or sheet of waxed paper. Phyllo dries out very quickly so cover pastry with plastic wrap or waxed paper and then a damp kitchen towel before using it as follows.

3. Preheat oven to 350°F [180°C]. Lay 1 sheet of phyllo vertically on a flat surface. Brush with melted butter, working from the centre of the sheet to the edges. Place another sheet of phyllo directly on top and brush with butter. Repeat with a third sheet of phyllo. [Alternatively, spray each sheet of phyllo lightly with olive oil.]

4. Using a sharp knife, cut phyllo into 3 equal vertical strips. Place about 1-1/2 Tbsp. [25 mL] of cooled spinach filling on the end of each strip. Fold over corner to make a triangle. Continue folding end to end to make a triangle-shaped envelope. Brush with melted butter to seal the seams and place in a single layer on a lightly greased, sprayed or parchment-lined baking sheet.

5. Working quickly, continue making spinach-stuffed phyllo triangles until all the spinach filling is used up. Be sure to cover the unused phyllo sheets with the damp cloth to prevent them from drying out as you work.

6. Bake until golden, about 15-20 minutes.

Serving suggestion: Serve 2 on a plate with a lightly tossed green salad for a tasty lunch.

Calories: 130; Protein 2.7 g; Carbohydrate 11.3 g; Fibre 1.6 g; Fat 8.4 g/serving [of 2 triangles made with butter]

Calories: 111; Protein 2.7 g; Carbohydrate 11 g; Fibre 1.6 g; Fat 6.2 g/serving [of 2 triangles made with olive oil and butter]

[pastas & sandwiches]

PHOTO: JOE BORRELLI

easy pasta toss

MAKES 4 TO 6 SERVINGS

3	Tbsp. [45 mL] oil from sun-dried tomatoes, divided
1	small onion, diced
3	garlic cloves, minced
3/4	lb. [375 g] fresh asparagus, cut into 1" [2.5 cm] pieces
1	each small red and yellow bell pepper, chunked
1/4	cup [60 mL] chopped oil-packed sun-dried tomatoes, drained
	Grated peel and juice of 1 lemon
3	Tbsp. [45 mL] drained capers
1/2	lb. [250 g] smoked Gouda cheese, diced
1	tsp. [5 mL] dried thyme
1	lb. [500 g] any pasta
	Salt and black pepper

Calories: 576;
Protein 24 g;
Carbohydrate 66 g;
Fibre 5.6 g;
Fat 24 g/serving

1. Have all vegetables prepared and the pasta on to cook in a large pot of salted water before you start.

2. In a large skillet, heat 1 Tbsp. [15 mL] tomato oil over medium-high heat; add onion and garlic; sauté for 2 minutes; add asparagus, bell peppers and tomatoes, stirring well.

3. Add 1/4 cup [60 mL] water to skillet, cover, steam vegetables for 2 minutes. Remove lid, stir-fry several minutes until liquid is absorbed and vegetables are tender-crisp.

4. Add lemon peel and juice, capers, cheese, thyme, salt and pepper and remaining tomato oil; stir well until heated through.

5. Meanwhile, drain the pasta when it gets to the al dente [tender but not mushy] stage. In a large bowl, toss together the hot pasta with the contents of the skillet.

6. Serve at once in heated pasta bowls.

Note: You can vary the vegetables you choose for this easy dish. The critical items are the sun-dried tomatoes [and their oil], the garlic and the thyme.

penne with tomatoes and basil

MAKES 4 TO 6 SERVINGS

2	Tbsp. [30 mL] olive oil
1	large onion, chopped
6	garlic cloves, minced
2	large carrots, diced
2	celery stalks with leaves, chopped
1	cup [250 mL] chopped fresh parsley
1	[28 fl. oz./796 mL] tin crushed tomatoes
1	[28 fl. oz./796 mL] tin diced tomatoes
2	Tbsp. [30 mL] Balsamic vinegar
1	[187 mL] bottle dry red wine
1/2	tsp. [3 mL] crushed red pepper flakes
1	tsp. [5 mL] salt
1	tsp. [5 mL] coarse black pepper
4	tsp. [20 mL] granulated sugar
1	Tbsp. [15 mL] Worcestershire sauce
2	[1/2 oz./14 g] pkgs. fresh basil, chopped
1	lb. [500 g] dry penne pasta
12	yellow [or red] cherry tomatoes, halved
	Shards of Asiago or Parmesan cheese

1. Heat oil in a large Dutch oven until hot; add onion, garlic, carrot and celery; sauté and stir occasionally for about 3 minutes.

2. Add the next 10 ingredients to the pot in the order listed, reducing the heat to a strong simmer. Stir occasionally while simmering for the next 2 hours.

3. At the end of 2 hours, add the chopped basil. Continue simmering another 3/4 hour.

4. Cook the penne in a large pot of salted boiling water until al dente. Drain [do not rinse] and return to pot.

5. Add the halved cherry tomatoes to the sauce; heat 1 minute. Add sauce to hot penne and toss to thoroughly coat the pasta.

6. Serve at once in large shallow pasta bowls with shards of cheese on top.

Serving suggestion: Great with sourdough bread and a hearts of Romaine salad.

Calories: 482;
Protein 14 g;
Carbohydrate 78 g;
Fibre 7.8 g;
Fat 8 g/serving

chicken tetrazzini casserole

MAKES 4 TO 6 SERVINGS

1-1/2	boneless, skinless chicken breasts
1	[187 mL] bottle dry white wine
2	[1/2 oz./14 g] pkgs. fresh sage, divided
6	large garlic cloves, halved
2	large carrots, peeled, thickly sliced
1	large onion, peeled, chunked
3/4	lb. [375 g] fresh angel hair or spaghetti pasta
3	Tbsp. [45 mL] butter or margarine
1/2	lb. [250 g] button mushrooms, sliced
3	Tbsp. [45 mL] all-purpose flour
1/2	tsp. [3 mL] dry English mustard
3/4	cup [175 mL] frozen peas
1/2	cup [125 mL] grated Gruyère [optional]
	Skim milk

Calories: 542;
Protein 37 g;
Carbohydrate 62 g;
Fibre 5 g;
Fat 14 g/serving

1. Place the chicken breasts and wine in a shallow baker with the leaves from one of the packages of sage and the halved garlic cloves. Cover with plastic wrap and microwave until chicken is just cooked. [Alternatively, poach the chicken in a saucepan on the stove, or in a baker in the oven.]

2. Remove the chicken; cut into large chunks; discard the sage leaves; mash the garlic cloves and set aside.

3. Measure the cooking liquid [there should be about 3/4 c./175 mL] and make it up to 2-1/2 cups [625 mL] with skim milk.

4. Add the carrots and onion to a large pot of salted boiling water; after 3-5 minutes, add pasta. Cook until pasta is just tender. Drain but do not rinse. Return to the pot.

5. Preheat oven to 350°F [180°C]. Meanwhile, in a medium saucepan, melt the butter or margarine until bubbly; add mushrooms and cook over high heat, stirring occasionally, until mushrooms are browned and have regained their liquid.

6. Reduce heat; stir in flour; stir 1 minute. Gradually stir in mustard and cooking liquid/milk mixture, cooking over medium heat until you have a smooth, thickened sauce.

7. Add mashed garlic, the other package of sage [chopped] and the peas; pour over the cooked carrots, onion and pasta; mix well to totally combine.

8. Place in a sprayed [or lightly greased] shallow 9" x 13" [23 x 30 cm] baker. Sprinkle the cheese over top, if using. Bake about 30 minutes or until bubbling; turn on broiler and place baker under heat for enough time to lightly brown the cheese on top.

Note: If you prepare the casserole ahead of time and refrigerate it, let it cook for a slightly longer period of time before putting it under the broiler.

PHOTO: JOHN SHERLOCK

asian rockshrimp ravioli

MAKES 4 APPETIZER SERVINGS

1	pkg. gyoza wrappers or round wonton wraps

Rockshrimp Filling:

1/2	lb. [250 g] rockshrimp or prawn meat
2	green onions, finely chopped
4	whole water chestnuts, finely chopped
4	Tbsp. [60 mL] finely chopped cilantro
1	Tbsp. [15mL] sesame oil
1	tsp. [5 mL] chili paste
1	garlic clove, minced

	Grated peel & juice of 1 lemon
1	egg
	Salt to taste

Citrus Soya Vinaigrette:

1/2	cup [125 mL] vegetable oil
1	Tbsp. [15 mL] sesame oil
1	large shallot, minced
4	Tbsp. [60 mL] rice wine vinegar
2	Tbsp. [30 mL] low-sodium soy sauce
	Grated peel & juice of 1 lemon
	Grated peel & juice of 1 lime
	Pepper to taste

1. For filling, mix all ingredients together [except egg] and taste for seasoning.

2. On a table, place 2 rows of 3 wrappers. Beat egg and use to brush edges of wrappers. Place 1 heaping Tbsp. [15 mL] of filling on first row of wrappers and use second row to cover. Pinch edges and remove all air, making sure to seal well. Place finished ravioli on parchment-lined baking sheet and cover with towel to prevent drying.

3. Continue with remaining ravioli. At this point, they may be frozen or used right away.

4. Whisk together or process vinaigrette ingredients and set aside.

5. Bring a large pot of salted water to a boil. Add ravioli one at a time. Make sure water is at a rapid boil or they will sink and stick together.

6. Drain and place 3 pieces on each plate. Drizzle vinaigrette on top and garnish with fresh cilantro, if desired.

Calories: 345;
Protein 18 g;
Carbohydrate 21 g;
Fibre 1.4 g;
Fat 22 g/serving

spring beans with angel hair pasta

MAKES 4 TO 6 SERVINGS

1-1/2	lbs. [750 g] green spring beans, trimmed top and bottom
3/4	lb. [375 g] dry angel hair pasta
4	Tbsp. [60 mL] olive oil, divided
4	ripe tomatoes, seeded, roughly chopped
1	[4.5 fl. oz./125 mL] tin sliced black olives, undrained
1	Tbsp. [15 mL] Balsamic vinegar
	Coarse black pepper
1/4	cup [60 mL] packed chopped fresh basil
1	[0.8 oz./22 g] pkg. Mayacamas Black Olive Pesto Skillet Toss Mix

Calories: 419;
Protein 11 g;
Carbohydrate 61 g;
Fibre 6.6 g;
Fat 15 g/serving

1. Bring a Dutch oven of salted water to the boil. Add beans and boil for 1-2 minutes. Remove with a slotted spoon.

2. Keep water boiling and add pasta. Cook as per package directions until tender but not over-cooked. Drain well, reserving about 1/2-3/4 cup [125-175 mL] of cooking water.

3. Meanwhile, heat 2 Tbsp. [30 mL] oil in a large skillet and add beans, tomatoes and olives. Stir-fry 1 minute.

4. Add vinegar and a generous amount of coarse black pepper. Remove pan from heat and add basil. Mix well.

5. Add Mayacamas Skillet Toss envelope contents to the hot drained pasta in the Dutch oven along with the remaining 2 Tbsp. [30 mL] oil and the reserved cooking water. Toss well.

6. Add contents of skillet to the Dutch oven. Toss everything together and serve at once on heated plates.

shrimp and spinach cannelloni

MAKES 4 TO 5 SERVINGS

6	oz. [180 g] fresh baby spinach, trimmed, dried, roughly chopped
1	lb. [500 g] fresh shrimp, roughly chopped
1	medium onion, minced or grated
3	Tbsp. [45 mL] chopped fresh parsley
2	garlic cloves, minced
1	cup [250 mL] 1% cottage cheese
8	fresh or precooked lasagne sheets

Sauce:

3	cups [750 mL] skim milk
3	bay leaves
4	parsley sprigs
1	small onion, chunked
1/4	cup [60 mL] butter
1/3	cup [75 mL] all-purpose flour
1/2	tsp. [3 mL] ground nutmeg
	Finely grated peel of 1/2 lemon
1/4	cup [60 mL] whipping cream
	Grated Parmesan cheese [optional]
	Salt and white pepper

1. Combine spinach, shrimp, minced onion, parsley, garlic and cottage cheese in a large bowl; mix well. Stir in a generous shaking of salt and pepper. Set aside.

2. Spray a shallow baking dish with vegetable oil cooking spray. [Size should be about 8" x 12"/20 x 30 cm.]

3. Cut each lasagne sheet in half so you have 16 pieces. Lay them flat on the counter. Spoon filling onto each, dividing it evenly among the 16 pieces. Roll up each into a tight roll and place in rows in the baking dish. You should have 4 rows of 4.

4. Preheat oven to 350°F [180°C]. Heat the skim milk, bay leaves, parsley sprigs and onion chunks in the microwave or in a small pan. Melt butter in a medium saucepan. When bubbly, stir in flour to make a smooth roux. Continue stirring one minute.

5. Gradually stir in the milk [pour it through a sieve to remove the flavouring ingredients]. Keep cooking and stirring until you have a smooth, thickened white sauce. Stir in nutmeg, peel, salt, white pepper and cream.

6. Pour evenly over cannelloni, making sure all rolls are covered with sauce. Sprinkle with grated Parmesan, if using.

7. Bake about 30-40 minutes or until bubbly and golden brown on top. Let sit 10 minutes before serving with a crisp salad or green vegetable.

Calories: 428;
Protein 36 g;
Carbohydrate 33 g;
Fibre 5.2 g;
Fat 16.4 g/serving

summer pasta

MAKES 6 SERVINGS

3	tomatoes, seeded, chopped
6"	[15 cm] English cucumber, unpeeled, chopped
1/4	cup [60 mL] packed basil leaves, washed, well dried
1/2	cup [125 mL] packed torn arugula leaves, washed, well dried
1	[8 oz./240 g] pkg. sugar snap peas, washed, well dried
4	sun-dried tomatoes in oil, diced
6	[12"/30 cm long] fresh lasagna sheets*

Dressing:

1	cup [250 mL] Ricotta cheese
3/4	cup [175 mL] plain low-fat yogurt
	Grated peel of 1 orange
	Juice of 1/2 lemon
1	Tbsp. [15 mL] liquid honey
3/4	tsp. [4 mL] coarse salt
3/4	tsp. [4 mL] coarse black pepper
	Minced fresh parsley [optional garnish]

Available in the deli department or the fresh pasta bar. Twelve cooked dry lasagna sheets can be substituted.

Calories: 179;
Protein 10.3 g;
Carbohydrate 4.3 g;
Fibre 1.8 g;
Fat 25.8 g/serving

1. Place 6 dinner plates in the refrigerator to chill.
2. Combine all vegetables [all well-dried] in a large bowl and mix well.
3. Drop the lasagna sheets into salted boiling water for one minute. [If using dry lasagna noodles, follow package directions to cook until al dente.] Drain well, rinse well in cold water, drain again and set aside.
4. Combine all dressing ingredients by whisking well or by using a hand-held blender.
5. Place chilled plates on the counter and drape one lasagna sheet [2 if you are using the smaller dried ones] over the plate. Pile the vegetable mixture on the pasta, top with dollops of the dressing and loop the lasagna sheet back and over top. The whole thing should look haphazard and casual – not formally rolled or filled.
6. Sprinkle minced parsley over each plate and serve at once with crusty bread and a glass of white wine.

spaghetti with arugula, roasted peppers and pecans
MAKES 4 TO 6 SERVINGS

1/3	cup [75 mL] chopped pecans, toasted
8	oz. [250 g] dry whole-wheat spaghetti
1	Tbsp. [15 mL] Western Family Olive Oil
4	garlic cloves, minced
1/8-1/4	tsp. [0.5-2 mL] crushed red pepper flakes
3	shallots, sliced
3	cups [750 mL] sliced baby mushrooms
1	roasted red bell pepper, seeded, julienned
1/4	cup [60 mL] white wine
8	oz. [250 g] arugula leaves, washed [about 8 cups/2 L]
2/3	cup [150 mL] freshly grated Asiago cheese, divided
1/2	tsp. [3 mL] ground black pepper

1. To toast nuts, preheat oven to 300°F [180°C]. Spread nuts on a baking sheet and bake 5-8 minutes, turning halfway through. Let cool.
2. Cook spaghetti in a large pot of salted boiling water until just tender, about 8-10 minutes.
3. Meanwhile, heat olive oil in a large non-stick skillet over medium heat. Add garlic and red pepper flakes; cook, stirring, until fragrant but not coloured, 1-2 minutes.
4. Add sliced shallots and mushrooms to the skillet; cook, stirring occasionally, until vegetables are tender, 3-5 minutes.
5. Stir in roasted pepper, wine and arugula; increase heat to medium-high. Cook, stirring often, until the arugula is wilted, about 1 minute.
6. Drain spaghetti and place in a large bowl. Add arugula mixture, half the Asiago cheese and the black pepper; toss until well combined. Sprinkle with toasted pecans and the remaining Asiago. Serve immediately.

Calories: 379; Protein 16 g; Carbohydrate 47 g; Fibre 6.8 g; Fat 16 g/serving

creamy tomato and
smoked salmon sauce in pasta nests

MAKES 4 SERVINGS

8	oz. [250 g] dry fettuccine
1	Tbsp. [15 mL] olive oil
1	Tbsp. [15 mL] butter
1/4	cooking onion, minced [about 2 Tbsp./30 mL]
1	large garlic clove, minced
2	ripe unpeeled tomatoes, diced
1	roasted red bell pepper, diced*
1/2	[125 g] pkg. low-fat cream cheese, cubed
1/3	cup [75 mL] 2% milk
2	oz. [60 g] sliced smoked salmon, diced
1/2	tsp. [3 mL] salt
	Freshly ground black pepper
1	Tbsp. [15 mL] capers, rinsed, drained
	Freshly grated Parmesan [optional]
	Fresh mint sprigs

*Roasted red bell peppers can be found in the deli department already peeled and seeded, or in the grocery aisle in a jar.

Calories: 412;
Protein 15 g;
Carbohydrate 55 g;
Fibre 3.8 g;
Fat 15 g/serving

1. Bring a large pot of water to a boil. Add pasta and stir until it remains separated. Boil uncovered for about 10 minutes or until tender to the bite. Remove from the heat. Drain and rinse.

2. Return to the pan and stir in the olive oil to prevent pasta from sticking. Cover to keep warm.

3. Meanwhile melt butter in a saucepan. Add minced onion and garlic and sauté over medium heat for 3-5 minutes or until softened. Stir often.

4. Add diced tomatoes, bell pepper, cubed cream cheese and milk. Using a wooden spoon, stir over medium heat to melt the cheese and blend all ingredients together.

5. Fold in diced smoked salmon. Add salt and pepper and continue to stir until piping hot. Remove from heat.

6. Using tongs, pinch up enough fettuccine for one serving and place on a warmed, single-serving pasta plate. Twirl pasta strands into a nest. Drizzle a desired amount of smoked salmon sauce over top. Repeat with remaining pasta and sauce.

7. Scatter a few capers over each serving and serve with freshly grated Parmesan on the side, if you wish, and garnish each serving with fresh mint.

creamy tomato
& smoked
salmon sauce
in pasta nests

thai
chicken
wraps

thai chicken wraps

MAKES 4 SERVINGS

4	Western Family Tortillas, 9" [23 cm] Burrito Style
1	tsp. [5 mL] canola oil
2	boneless, skinless chicken breast halves, cut into thin strips
1	cup [250 mL] each bean sprouts, halved snow peas and sliced red bell pepper
1/2	cup [125 mL] Western Classics Thai Cooking Sauce
1	cup [250 mL] hot cooked rice, divided
3/4	cup [175 mL] grated carrots

1. To warm tortillas, wrap in a damp kitchen towel and place in a 250°F [120°C] oven for 10 minutes; or cover with a paper towel and microwave 2 at a time on high for 30 seconds.

2. Meanwhile, heat oil in a large, non-stick wok or skillet over medium-high heat. Add chicken. Cook and stir until chicken is lightly browned and no longer pink.

3. Add bean sprouts, snow peas and red pepper. Cook for 2 more minutes.

4. Add Thai sauce. Cook until sauce is bubbly. Remove from heat.

5. To assemble wraps, place a warm tortilla on a serving plate. Spoon 1/4 rice in centre, followed by 1/4 of grated carrots. Spoon 1/4 hot chicken/vegetable mixture over top. Fold bottom of tortilla up to cover part of filling, then fold in sides. Serve immediately.

Time-savers: Ready-made sauces, dressings and marinades make for tasty shortcut solutions to add sizzle to any meal. From classic salad dressings to Asian-influenced marinades, to luscious Italian pasta sauces, today's inspired bottled blends can place a world of flavour at your fingertips.

Calories: 368;
Protein 21 g;
Carbohydrate 56 g;
Fibre 2.6 g;
Fat 6.1 g/serving

spicy asian beef in tortillas

MAKES 4 SERVINGS

5	Tbsp. [75 mL] vegetable oil, divided
1	tsp. [5 mL] sesame oil
2	garlic cloves, minced
1	Tbsp. [15 mL] minced ginger root
1	Tbsp. [15 mL] toasted sesame seeds*
3	Tbsp. [45 mL] finely chopped green onion
3	Tbsp. [45 mL] finely chopped cilantro
3	Tbsp. [45 mL] low-sodium soy sauce
1	Jalapeño, seeded, finely minced
1	tsp. [5 mL] granulated sugar
2	Tbsp. [30 mL] dry sherry [optional]
1-1/2	lb. [750 g] sirloin steak, trimmed, cut into 1/2" [1.25 cm] strips
1	large onion, julienned
1/2	large red bell pepper, julienned
1/2	large green bell pepper, julienned
4	[8"/20 cm] flour tortillas
	Hot mashed potatoes [optional]
	Cilantro sprigs [optional]
	Green onions [optional]

*To toast seeds: spread seeds on a baking sheet in a preheated 350°F [180°C] oven.
Bake about 10-15 minutes, stirring once or twice until lightly browned.

Calories: 525;
Protein 45 g;
Carbohydrate 28 g;
Fibre 3.1 g;
Fat 25 g/serving
[without potatoes]

1. In a large bowl, mix together 2 Tbsp. [30 mL] vegetable oil, sesame oil, garlic, ginger, sesame seeds, green onion, cilantro, soy sauce, Jalapeño, sugar and dry sherry. Add beef strips; toss together to coat beef completely; cover; marinate for one hour.

2. Heat remaining oil in a large saucepan over medium-high heat until bubbly; add onion, peppers and marinated beef. Sauté until beef strips are just medium rare.

3. Wrap the tortillas in foil and warm in oven [or wrap in paper towel and warm in microwave]. Divide meat mixture evenly among the warmed tortillas; fold or roll to serve. Garnish with cilantro sprigs or green onions, if desired.

Serving suggestion: Spread a scoop of hot mashed potatoes over the tortillas before adding the beef mixture.

chicken and basmati pita pockets

MAKES 4 SERVINGS

2	large whole skinless, boneless chicken breasts
2	garlic cloves, minced
1	tsp. [5 mL] minced ginger root
1	cup [250 mL] strained low-fat yogurt*
1/2	tsp. [3 mL] ground cumin
1/2	tsp. [3 mL] ground coriander
1	tsp. [5 mL] ground turmeric
1/4	tsp. [2 mL] cayenne
2	cups [500 mL] raw Basmati rice, cooked
3	Tbsp. [45 mL] chopped fresh mint
3	Tbsp. [45 mL] chopped cilantro
3	Tbsp. [45 mL] chopped green onion
4	whole pitas, cut in half to make 8 pockets
	Chopped red onion [optional]
	Cilantro sprigs [optional]
	Bamboo skewers, soaked in water

Yogurt Sauce:

1	cup [250 mL] low-fat plain or vanilla yogurt
1	garlic clove, minced
1	Tbsp. [15 mL] curry powder
2	Tbsp. [30 mL] chopped cilantro

*To strain yogurt, pour yogurt into a strainer covered with cheesecloth. Cover and drain over a bowl for up to 4 hours. Keep refrigerated during this time.

---

1. Cut chicken breasts into 1" [2.5 cm] chunks; place in a medium bowl.
2. In a small bowl, mix together garlic, ginger, strained yogurt, cumin, coriander, turmeric and cayenne. Pour marinade over chicken; mix; allow to marinate for 1 hour.
3. Preheat broiler or barbecue.
4. Skewer marinated chicken pieces onto soaked bamboo skewers; cook under broiler or on barbecue until done, about 5 minutes, turning once. Baste with any leftover marinade while cooking. Discard any unused marinade.
5. In a medium bowl, mix together hot cooked Basmati rice, mint, cilantro and green onion.
6. To make raita [yogurt sauce]: in a small bowl mix together all sauce ingredients.
7. To serve, separate and open pita halves to form pockets; add scoop of the herbed Basmati rice, skewer of chicken [pulling out skewer]; drizzle over yogurt sauce. Add chopped red onion and cilantro sprigs for garnish, if desired.

Calories: 729;
Protein 50 g;
Carbohydrate 121 g;
Fibre 1.6 g;
Fat 5 g/serving

portobello and basil sandwiches on focaccia

MAKES 8 SANDWICHES

8	slices lean bacon
1	focaccia wheel [about 2"/30 cm in diameter]
2	garlic cloves, minced
5	large Portobello mushrooms
1	Tbsp. [15 mL] Balsamic vinegar
2	[1/2 oz./14 g] pkg. fresh basil leaves*
	Dijonnaise sandwich spread

*Or use an equivalent amount of fresh basil plant leaves. If you are really fond of basil, use more.

Calories: 252;
Protein 8 g;
Carbohydrate 37 g;
Fibre 0.8 g;
Fat 8 g/serving

1. Place bacon in a large skillet and cook until crisp; remove from pan and keep warm.
2. In 2 Tbsp. [30 mL] of fat remaining in the pan, cook garlic 1 minute over medium heat.
3. Remove stems from mushrooms [they can be put into your stock pot] and cut each mushroom into 4 or 5 pieces. Add pieces to the skillet; toss and cook about 2 to 3 minutes or until they are tender and browned on both sides.
4. Meanwhile, heat broiler. Cut focaccia wheel into 8 wedges; slice the wedges in half, horizontally. Place pieces on a baking tray and broil on both sides until lightly golden.
5. Spread both bottoms and tops with Dijonnaise. Place pieces of Portobello, covered with garlic on the bottoms. Top each with lots of fresh basil leaves. Top each with a piece of crisp bacon; replace the top wedges to make the sandwiches. Serve at once.

grilled caesar steak sandwich
MAKES 4 SERVINGS

4	favourite 4 oz. [125 g] steaks [such as Western Family New York Strip Loins or eye of the round]
1/2	cup [125 mL] low-fat plain yogurt
	Grated peel and juice of 1 small lemon
1	Tbsp. [15 mL] granulated sugar
1	Tbsp. [15 mL] Worcestershire sauce
3	garlic cloves, minced
1/2	Tbsp. [8 mL] Dijon mustard
1/2	Tbsp. [8 mL] anchovy paste
1/2	Tbsp. [8 mL] drained capers
1/2	Tbsp. [8 mL] red wine vinegar
1/4	cup [60 mL] olive oil
1	large onion, cut into thick slices
	Romaine lettuce leaves, washed, torn
	Grated Parmesan cheese [optional]
4	long crusty rolls or 4 large Kaiser buns or 8 thick slices of French bread

1. Trim all visible fat from the steaks; place in a shallow, non-metallic baker.

2. Combine next 10 ingredients using a food processor or a handheld blender to make a dressing. Pour 3/4 cup [175 mL] dressing over steaks, turning them several times to coat. Cover with plastic wrap; refrigerate overnight. Cover and refrigerate remaining dressing overnight.

3. Remove all items from the refrigerator.

4. Preheat the barbecue to medium-high heat. Barbecue the onion and steaks to desired degree of doneness, brushing both with the marinade as you cook. Let steaks sit 5-10 minutes after cooking to retain juices.

5. Meanwhile, place torn Romaine lettuce leaves [about 4 or 5] in a small bowl; toss with enough of the remaining dressing [not the marinade] to make a small "Caesar Salad," adding 2 Tbsp. [30 mL] of grated Parmesan if you wish.

6. Place split buns or bread slices on the barbecue to grill one side; spread remaining dressing on the buns.

7. To serve: Place a steak on each bun, topping with onion slices and some Romaine salad. Top each with top of bun or another slice of grilled bread. Serve at once.

Calories: 384;
Protein 33 g;
Carbohydrate 27 g;
Fibre 2 g;
Fat 16 g/serving

chicken salad buns

MAKES 4 BUNS

3	cups [750 mL] chopped cooked chicken
1	[4.5 fl. oz./125 mL] tin sliced black olives, drained
2	Tbsp. [30 mL] minced sun-dried tomatoes [well-drained of oil]
2	green onions, chopped
3	celery stalks, diced
2	Tbsp. [30 mL] tarragon Dijon mustard
1/4	cup [60 mL] low-fat yogurt or sour cream
4	Kaiser buns
	Mixed baby spring greens*

*Available in bulk in the produce department or already washed in bags.

Calories: 563;
Protein 79 g;
Carbohydrate 21 g;
Fibre 1.6 g;
Fat 16 g/sandwich

1. Combine all ingredients [except the buns and greens] in a bowl and mix well.
2. Spread on the bottom bun halves. Top each with a generous handful of greens and place bun tops on each sandwich. Cut buns in half to serve.

Serving suggestion: Add different flavours and textures to this sandwich by using a variety of different buns each time you serve it.

the ultimate grilled three-cheese sandwich
MAKES 4 SERVINGS

2	Tbsp. [30 mL] commercially prepared sun-dried tomato pesto
4	Tbsp. [60 mL] plain Chèvre [goat cheese]
8	slices sourdough bread
4	[3/4 oz./20 g] slices Raclette or Fontina cheese
4	[3/4 oz./20 g] slices Provolone or Mozzarella cheese
	Fresh chopped basil
	Spinach leaves, washed and spun dry

1. Combine pesto and Chèvre in a small bowl; stir together to blend. Spread even amounts on 4 slices of sourdough bread.

2. Cover each slice with several spinach leaves. Top each with a slice each of Raclette and Provolone, overlapping as needed to prevent cheese from hanging over. Sprinkle with basil as desired.

3. Top with second slice of sourdough. Place a heavy skillet over low heat. Spray with a little nonstick vegetable cooking spray. Wait 30 seconds, then add sandwich. Using a flat cover that fits inside the pan, press down on sandwich occasionally.

4. Grill, turning a couple of times with a spatula until cheese is melted and sandwich is golden, about 5 minutes. Place sandwiches in a warm oven as they are grilled and repeat with remaining sandwiches. Serve immediately.

Serving suggestion: Try varying the cheese combinations for different flavours. This recipe uses four cow's milk cheeses, each of which contributes its own unique taste. Fontina is pale yellow with a red waxed rind and nutty flavour. Raclette is mellower in taste and traditionally enjoyed melted. Mozzarella is a mild white cheese with an elastic texture that is ideal for melting, while pale-yellow Italian Provolone is a firmer cheese.

Calories: 192;
Protein 8.2 g;
Carbohydrate 27 g;
Fibre 3.3 g;
Fat 5.5 g/serving

crab/shrimp sandwiches with ginger and lemon

MAKES 8 TO 10 SANDWICHES

1	lb. [500 g] artificial crab or fresh shrimp/crab
1/2	cup [125 mL] minced green bell pepper
1/4	cup [60 mL] minced water chestnuts
1	stalk celery, minced
1	Tbsp. [15 mL] minced fresh ginger root
1/3	cup [75 mL] minced bean sprouts
	Grated peel and juice of 1 lemon
1/3	cup [75 mL] thick Sour Cream and Chive Dressing*
	Favourite buns, French bread, mini focaccias, whole-wheat bread, etc.
	Swiss cheese slices [optional]

*Try any Western Classics thick dressing with compatible flavours [regular or light].

Calories: 240;
Protein 15.5 g;
Carbohydrate 31.5 g;
Fibre 1 g;
Fat 6 g/serving

1. Chop or mince the chosen seafood; place in a large bowl. Add remaining ingredients except for the dressing, bread and cheese; mix well. [Do not add dressing until you are ready to serve the sandwiches.]
2. Choose the bread or buns, etc., you are using; spread on seafood mixture.
3. Serve sandwiches or buns cold, or broil one side of slices of bread or tops and bottoms of split buns or focaccia; top untoasted sides with the seafood mixture, then a slice of Swiss cheese; broil to melt cheese.
4. Serve with sliced tomato, red onion and fresh basil on the side if desired.

PHOTO: JOE BORRELLI

curried shrimp rolls

MAKES 6 ROLLS

3/4	cup [175 mL] raw long grain or Basmati rice
2	cups [500 mL] water
1	ripe mango
1/4	cup [60 mL] light mayonnaise
1	shallot, chopped
6-8	drops Tabasco
1/2	tsp. [3 mL] granulated sugar
1-1/2	tsp. [8 mL] curry powder
1	lb. [500 g] cooked baby shrimp
2	ripe avocados
	Juice of 1 small lemon
6	[9"/23 cm] spinach or sun-dried tomato wraps
	Salt and pepper, to taste

1. Combine rice, water and salt in a pan. Bring to the boil, then reduce heat and simmer [covered] 15 minutes [or use leftover cold rice from another meal].

2. While rice is cooking, halve the mango and cut the fruit from the skin into bite-size pieces.

3. Combine mango flesh, mayonnaise, shallot, salt and pepper, Tabasco, sugar and curry in a food processor or mini-chop and process until smooth.

4. Combine shrimp and cooled rice in a bowl. Mix in mango dressing.

5. Mash avocados in a small bowl with the lemon juice. Spread avocado over the surface of all 6 wraps, out to the edges. Spread the shrimp and rice mixture on top. Roll tightly and wrap in plastic. Refrigerate for about 2 hours.

6. Slice each roll in half diagonally and tilt the cut halves over piles of mixed greens for an elegant luncheon presentation. Or cut each roll into 6-8 slices to serve as appetizers.

Calories: 439;
Protein 23 g;
Carbohydrate 50 g;
Fibre 4.2 g;
Fat 16 g/roll

[vegetables & side dishes]

Three-Mustard Asparagus Spears
Spicy Thai Rice
Basil, Roasted Pepper and Tomato Toss
Brussels Sprouts and Cauliflower Medley
Scalloped Potatoes
Carrots Provençal
Nugget Potatoes with Pesto
Oven-Roasted Autumn Vegetables with Cider Glaze
Risotto alla Milanese
Spicy Seeded Pilaf with Okra and Spinach
Garlicky Beans and Greens
Broccoli Soufflé
Garlic Roast Beets
Potatoes au Gratin
Swiss Chard Sautéed with Pine Nuts
Broccoli and Carrot Bake

three-mustard asparagus spears

MAKES 4 SERVINGS

1	egg
1/2	cup [125 mL] mayonnaise*
2-1/2	tsp. [12 mL] grainy mustard
1-1/2	tsp. [8 mL] dry English mustard
1	tsp. [5 mL] Dijon mustard
1	tsp. [5 mL] fresh lemon juice
1	tsp. [5 mL] liquid honey
2	Tbsp. [30 mL] dry white wine
1	lb. [500 g] fresh asparagus spears

*Low-fat sour cream can be used instead of mayonnaise but the sauce will be thinner and will not coat the asparagus as well.

Calories: 260;
Protein 4 g;
Carbohydrate 5 g;
Fibre 2.8 g;
Fat 25 g/serving

1. Hard-cook egg shortly before making sauce, placing in ice water to cool while you prepare sauce and asparagus.
2. Combine all other ingredients except asparagus in a small microwave-proof bowl; cover loosely with plastic wrap; microwave on medium [50%] power about 4-5 minutes, stirring once, until hot.
3. Meanwhile, chop hard-cooked egg.
4. Cook asparagus [see asparagus tips below], drain and place portions on heated plates. Serve with sauce over top and egg sprinkled over.

Asparagus tips: The best cooking method is to tie the spears together with string and cook upright in a tall pot of boiling water; the water covers the stems and the tips are cooked by the steam. Cook quickly and only until bright green in colour. Drain and the residual heat will complete the cooking process.

spicy thai rice

MAKES 4 TO 6 SERVINGS

1	cup [250 mL] Basmati rice*
2	tsp. [10 mL] vegetable oil
2	tsp. [10 mL] grated fresh ginger root
4	garlic cloves, minced
1	small onion, chopped
1	small red bell pepper, seeded, diced
1-1/2	cups [375 mL] chicken broth
1-2	Jalapeños, seeded, minced
3	Tbsp. [45 mL] oyster sauce
2-3	Tbsp. [30-45 mL] hot Szechuan paste
1	Tbsp. [15 mL] sesame oil
1/4	lb. [125 g] firm tofu, diced [optional]
3	Tbsp. [45 mL] chopped cilantro
	Grated peel and juice of 1 lime

*Any long grain white rice can be substituted.

1. Cover rice with cold water in a small saucepan; let stand 1/2 hour; drain.
2. Meanwhile, prepare all ingredients.
3. Heat oil in wok or large skillet with a lid. When bubbly, add ginger, garlic and onion; stir-fry 30 seconds.
4. Add drained rice; stir well to coat rice.
5. Add red pepper and broth; stir; reduce heat to simmer; cover with lid. Set timer for 20 minutes.
6. Remove lid; stir; add all remaining ingredients; stir to mix well; stir-fry 1 minute.
7. Serve at once with a Thai meal.

Calories 275;
Protein 10 g;
Carbohydrate 43 g;
Fibre 2 g;
Fat 7 g/serving
with tofu

basil, roasted pepper and tomato toss

MAKES 4 ENTRÉE SERVINGS OR 8 SIDE DISH SERVINGS

2	red bell peppers
1	yellow bell pepper
4	ripe Roma tomatoes
9	small red or nugget potatoes
2	Tbsp. [30 mL] extra-virgin olive oil
3	garlic cloves, minced
2	green onions, chopped
1	tsp. [5 mL] coarse black pepper
1/2	tsp. [3 mL] salt
2	[1/2 oz./14 g] pkgs. fresh basil leaves, roughly chopped*
1	cup [250 mL] Asiago shards

*Or use an equivalent amount of fresh basil plant leaves.

Calories: 408;
Protein 16 g;
Carbohydrate 50 g;
Fibre 5.3 g;
Fat 16 g/entrée serving

Calories: 204;
Protein 8 g;
Carbohydrate 25 g;
Fibre 2.6 g;
Fat 8 g/side dish
serving

1. Cut peppers and tomatoes in half; clean out insides of peppers. Place all, cut-side down, on a baking tray and place under the broiler. Broil until the peppers are black and the tomatoes' skins have split. Place the peppers in a paper bag for about 30 minutes; then peel off skin and roughly chop. Remove skins from tomatoes and roughly chop.

2. Meanwhile, scrub potatoes; cut each into halves or quarters; cook in microwave or in a saucepan. When just tender, drain.

3. Heat the oil in a large skillet until bubbly. Add garlic and green onion; toss and cook 30 seconds. Stir in large pieces of bell pepper and tomato, potato chunks, pepper and salt.

4. Toss and cook about 2 to 3 minutes; add basil; toss and cook 1 minute.

5. Serve on hot plates with shards of Asiago cheese scattered over each serving, just melting into the mixture.

brussels sprouts and cauliflower medley

MAKES 6 SERVINGS

3/4	lb. [375 g] tiny brussels sprouts, halved
3/4	lb. [375 g] cauliflower florets
2	Tbsp. [30 mL] oil
2	large garlic cloves, peeled, halved
1	small onion, diced
1	small red bell pepper, seeded, diced
1/2	tsp. [3 mL] salt
1/2	tsp. [3 mL] white pepper
1	Tbsp. [15 mL] grated lemon peel
1/2	lemon, sliced
	Chopped fresh parsley

1. Trim brussels sprouts and cauliflower pieces until you have bite-sized pieces of each. Place in a steamer or boiling water and cook only until just tender crisp – brussels sprouts should still be bright green. [This can also be done in the microwave.] Drain completely.

2. Heat oil in a large skillet; add garlic pieces and toss over medium heat until garlic browns. Discard garlic.

3. Add onion and red pepper to hot garlic oil. Toss until onion is tender and slightly golden – do not overcook.

4. Add par-cooked brussels sprouts and cauliflower pieces, salt, pepper, lemon peel and lemon slices. Toss and cook until heated through and vegetables are tender.

5. Discard lemon slices and serve at once in a heated vegetable dish.

Calories: 109;
Protein 4 g;
Carbohydrate 12 g;
Fibre 4.9 g;
Fat 5 g/serving

scalloped potatoes

MAKES 4 TO 6 SERVINGS

3	Tbsp. [45 mL] butter or margarine
3	Tbsp. [45 mL] all-purpose flour
1	cup [250 mL] 1% milk
1	tsp. [5 mL] dry mustard
1/4	tsp. [1 mL] salt
1/4	tsp. [1 mL] coarse black pepper
2	tsp. [10 mL] chopped fresh thyme
1	[10 fl. oz./284 mL tin] half-fat chicken broth
2-1/2	lbs. [1.25 kg] baking potatoes
1	large onion, thinly sliced
1/2	cup [125 mL] grated light Gruyère cheese
1/2	cup [125 mL] grated light "old" Cheddar cheese

Calories: 307;
Protein 13 g;
Carbohydrate 39 g;
Fibre 3.9 g;
Fat 11 g/serving
[version 1]

Calories: 262;
Protein 12 g;
Carbohydrate 40 g;
Fat 6 g/serving
[version 2]

.

1. Preheat oven to 350°F [180°C].

2. Lightly grease or spray a 9" x 13" [23 x 30 cm] shallow baker.

3. Heat butter or margarine in a medium saucepan until hot; stir in flour to make a smooth roux. Cook 30 seconds, stirring constantly. Gradually stir in milk, seasonings and broth. Stir and cook until you have a smooth, thickened sauce. Remove from heat.

4. Peel potatoes only when you are ready to assemble the dish. Slice potatoes very thinly [on a mandolin or similar slicer]. Place a single layer of potato slices in the bottom of the baker. Top with a layer of onion rings. Repeat potatoes and onions until you have only one layer of potatoes left. Sprinkle with grated Gruyère.

5. Now add the final layer of potatoes. Pour the sauce evenly over the casserole. Sprinkle the grated Cheddar over top of all layers.

6. Place baker in the middle of the oven. Bake uncovered for about 1 hour or until potatoes are tender and sauce has been mostly absorbed by the potatoes. The dish should still be "saucy" in texture, not dry. Serve at once.

Variation: For a faster version, use 1 tin [10 fl. oz./284 mL] half-fat cream of mushroom soup and 1 tin [10 fl. oz./284 mL] 1% milk instead of the sauce above. Assemble and bake the dish in exactly the same manner as above.

carrots provençal

MAKES 6 TO 8 SERVINGS

2	lbs. [1 kg] carrots [about 12 medium]
2	Tbsp. [30 mL] olive oil
1	whole head garlic, cloves separated, peeled
	Salt and freshly ground pepper, to taste
1/2	cup [125 mL] black olives, pitted
1/2	cup [125 mL] finely chopped fresh dill

1. Peel carrots and slice on the diagonal into 1/4" [0.6 cm] slices.

2. In a large skillet with a tight-fitting lid, heat oil over medium heat. Add carrots; stir to coat with oil and lower heat to medium-low. Cover and cook for about 20 minutes, stirring often.

3. Slice garlic cloves in half; add to carrots, season with salt and pepper and reduce heat to low. Cook until carrots are caramelized and garlic is softened, about 15 minutes.

4. Stir in the olives and dill to thoroughly combine and heat; serve at once.

Garlic primer: A key component in this recipe, garlic is one of the cooking world's most enduring ingredients. When cooking with garlic remember that its distinctive taste and pungent scent are released only after the cloves are exposed to the air through cutting, crushing or chopping; using raw garlic will produce a dish with very strong flavour. Cooking or roasting garlic significantly mellows both its taste and aroma. Can you believe that adding 40 cloves of garlic to a chicken while roasting will actually produce a less garlicky dish than crushing five raw cloves and adding them to mayonnaise?

Calories: 122;
Protein 1.9 g;
Carbohydrate 17 g;
Fibre 3 g;
Fat 6.1 g/serving

nugget potatoes with pesto

MAKES 6 SERVINGS

2	lbs. [1 kg] nugget potatoes, scrubbed, halved or quartered
1/2	cup [125 mL] each packed basil leaves and packed parsley
4	whole peeled garlic cloves
2	Tbsp. [30 mL] pine nuts
1/4	cup [60 mL] julienned sun-dried tomatoes, drained
1-1/2	tsp. [8 mL] coarse black pepper
1-1/4	tsp. [6 mL] salt
1/4	cup [60 mL] extra virgin olive oil
	Grated Parmesan [optional]

Calories: 241;
Protein 5 g;
Carbohydrate 30 g;
Fibre 3.3 g;
Fat 12 g/serving

1. Drop the potato chunks into salted boiling water and cook until tender but not mushy. Drain.

2. Meanwhile, combine all remaining ingredients except Parmesan in a food processor and process until well combined. Recipe makes about 10 Tbsp. pesto [150 mL]. Use desired amount to toss with the potatoes in this recipe; cover and refrigerate the remainder for up to 3 days for another use.

3. Return the drained potatoes to the hot pan in which they were cooked and add desired amount of pesto [about 1/2 to 3/4]. Toss until hot potatoes are well coated.

4. Sprinkle with grated Parmesan if desired. Serve at once.

Note: This recipe makes more pesto than required, but leftover pesto is excellent beaten into mashed potatoes, or spread under the skin of chicken breasts or legs.

nugget
potatoes
with pesto

oven-roasted
autumn
vegetables
with cider
glaze

oven-roasted autumn vegetables with cider glaze

MAKES 6 SERVINGS

1	lb. [500 g] butternut squash, peeled, seeded, cut into 2" [5 cm] pieces
1	bunch small beets, peeled, cut into 2" [5 cm] pieces
1	medium red onion, peeled, cut into 8 wedges
1	red bell pepper, halved, seeded, cut into 2" [5 cm] pieces
6	carrots, peeled, cut into 2" [5 cm] pieces
1	fennel bulb, trimmed, cut into 8 wedges
1	whole garlic, separated, peeled
2	Tbsp. [30 mL] olive oil
	Salt and freshly ground black pepper
	Fresh rosemary sprigs [optional]

Cider Glaze:

1/4	cup [60 mL] apple cider or juice
1/4	cup [60 mL] water or vegetable broth
1	Tbsp. [15 mL] unsalted butter
2	Tbsp. [30 mL] maple syrup
5	fresh thyme sprigs

1. Preheat oven to 400°F [200°C].

2. Line a large rimmed baking sheet with aluminum foil.

3. Combine the prepared vegetables, olive oil and salt and pepper to taste in a large bowl; toss to coat. Transfer vegetables to prepared baking sheet; spread out evenly and tuck in the rosemary sprigs if using. Roast vegetables until tender, stirring occasionally, for about 45 minutes to 1 hour. [Vegetables can be prepared up to 2 hours ahead and reheated in a 350°F/180°C oven for 15-20 minutes.]

4. Meanwhile, make the cider glaze: In a small saucepan combine the apple cider, water or vegetable broth, butter, maple syrup and thyme. Bring to a boil, reduce the heat to medium and cook, uncovered, for about 10 minutes or until reduced by half.

5. Season to taste with salt and pepper. Transfer the cooked vegetables to a serving bowl and toss with the glaze. Serve immediately.

*Calories: 212;
Protein 4 g;
Carbohydrate 37 g;
Fibre 5.9 g;
Fat 7 g/serving*

side dish

PHOTO: JOHN SHERLOCK

risotto alla milanese

MAKES 4 SERVINGS

6-7	cups [1.5-1.75 L] chicken broth
1	large pinch saffron threads
1/4	cup [60 mL] butter
1	medium onion, finely chopped
3-4	garlic cloves, minced
2	cups [500 mL] Italian arborio rice
1/2	cup [125 mL] dry white wine
1	cup [250 mL] grated Parmesan-Reggiano cheese
1/4	cup [60 mL] whipping cream [optional]
	Salt and black pepper to taste

*Calories: 673;
Protein 26 g;
Carbohydrate 86 g;
Fibre 2.2 g;
Fat 22 g/serving
[without whipping
cream]*

1. In a saucepan, bring the chicken broth to a simmer over high heat, then reduce and keep at a simmer while cooking the rice.
2. Mix the saffron with 1/2 cup [125 mL] hot broth and allow to infuse for a couple of minutes.
3. In a heavy saucepan, melt the butter over medium-high heat; add the onion and stir until translucent, about 5 minutes [do not burn]. Add the garlic and rice and stir until all the grains are well coated, about 2 minutes. Add the wine and stir until all of it has evaporated.
4. Add half of the saffron-infused broth and add 1/2 cup [125 mL] of the hot broth and stir until most of it has evaporated. Continue adding the hot broth in 1/2 cup [125 mL] amounts until most of the liquid has been absorbed and the rice is tender with a slight al dente texture.
5. Add the remaining saffron-infused broth halfway through cooking. Adjust the heat if too hot and the liquid is evaporating too quickly – it should be simmering.
6. When the rice is cooked, add the cheese and stir until mixed thoroughly. For a richer and creamier texture, add whipping cream. Season to taste with salt and freshly ground pepper.
7. Serve with additional grated Parmesan cheese.

PHOTO: JOHN SHERLOCK

spicy seeded pilaf with okra and spinach

MAKES 4 SERVINGS

1	medium onion, cut into thin strips
1/2	lb. [250 g] pattypan squash, halved*
1-1/2	tsp. [8 mL] hot chili powder
1/2	tsp. [3 mL] turmeric
2	Tbsp. [30 mL] vegetable oil
1	tsp. [5 mL] mustard seeds
1	tsp. [5 mL] cumin seeds, crushed
1	tsp. [5 mL] coriander seeds, crushed
4	garlic cloves, minced
1/4	tsp. [2 mL] salt
1	cup [250 mL] white Basmati rice
2	cups [500 mL] hot vegetable or chicken broth
2	dried bay leaves
1/4	cup [60 mL] coconut cream [not milk]
1/2	cup [125 mL] rinsed and chopped okra
1/4	lb. [125 g] baby spinach, dried
1/2	cup [125 mL] fresh or frozen green peas
1/2	cup [125 mL] shredded unsweetened coconut

*Look for the small, flat, disc-shaped squash in the produce section.

1. In a mixing bowl, toss onion and pattypan squash with chili powder and turmeric.
2. Heat the oil in a saucepan over medium-high heat and add the squash and onions; sauté 1-2 minutes or until fragrant.
3. Add the mustard seeds, cumin, coriander, garlic and salt. Reduce heat and cook over moderate heat until the seeds begin to crackle and pop and become aromatic.
4. Stir in the rice and sauté another minute; stirring gently, add the hot broth, bay leaves and coconut cream. Cover and reduce heat to simmering, then cook undisturbed for 8 minutes.
5. Stir in the okra, spinach, peas and coconut. Cover and cook a further 4-5 minutes or until the rice is tender. Remove the bay leaves and stir well to mix thoroughly.

Calories: 399;
Protein 10 g;
Carbohydrate 56 g;
Fibre 6 g;
Fat 16 g/serving

garlicky beans and greens

MAKES 6 SERVINGS

1	lb. [500 g] fresh green beans, trimmed
1/4	cup [60 mL] olive oil
	Juice of 1/2 lemon
3	garlic cloves, minced
1	Tbsp. [15 mL] fresh chopped sage or
1	tsp. [5 mL] dried sage
1/8	tsp. [0.5 mL] salt
	Freshly ground black pepper
2	fresh ripe tomatoes, diced
1	head radicchio
4	Belgian endive
2	oz. [60 g] shaved Parmesan cheese

Calories 173;
Protein 6.5 g;
Carbohydrate 12.6 g;
Fibre 7 g;
Fat 12 g/serving

1. Preheat oven to 450°F [230°C].

2. Place cleaned and trimmed beans in a large bowl.

3. Combine olive oil, lemon juice, garlic and seasonings in a small bowl. Whisk to blend. Add to beans and toss to coat evenly.

4. Add tomatoes. Transfer to a 3 qt. [3 L] baking dish. Bake for 10 minutes. Stir often.

5. Meanwhile, wash and dry radicchio. Tear into bite-size pieces.

6. Wash Belgian endive and separate the leaves. Combine with radicchio and arrange on a large platter.

7. When beans are tender-crisp, remove from the oven. Spoon beans and sauce over chilled salad greens. Garnish with shaved Parmesan and serve.

broccoli soufflé

MAKES 3 TO 4 SERVINGS

3/4	lb. [375 g] fresh broccoli
5	Tbsp. [75 mL] butter
2	shallots, minced
1/4	cup [60 mL] all-purpose flour
1	cup [250 mL] chicken broth
5	eggs, separated
1/2	tsp. [3 mL] black pepper
1	Tbsp. [15 mL] Dijon mustard
1	Tbsp. [15 mL] Worcestershire sauce
1/2	cup [125 mL] shredded [not grated] Parmesan cheese
	Dash cayenne

1. Dice the broccoli stems into a 1/4" [0.6 cm] dice and place in a bowl with loose plastic covering. Microwave on high power for 2 minutes.

2. Chop broccoli heads into tiny pieces and add to bowl. Replace covering and microwave on high power another 2 minutes. Remove plastic and drain off any liquid in the bottom of the bowl.

3. Preheat oven to 375°F [190°C]. Heat butter in a medium saucepan until bubbly. Add shallots and sauté until soft.

4. Stir in flour and cook, stirring, 1 minute. Stir in broth and cook, stirring, until smooth.

5. Remove from heat and stir in egg yolks, one at a time. Stir in pepper, cayenne, Dijon and Worcestershire.

6. Add par-cooked broccoli stems and tops and the shredded Parmesan. Mix well and set aside to cool slightly.

7. Beat the egg whites in a large bowl until stiff. Stir about 1/4 of them gently into the broccoli sauce to lighten it. Fold the lightened sauce into the remaining egg whites, leaving lots of white showing.

8. Gently transfer the soufflé mixture to a 2 qt. [2 L] soufflé dish. Place in the middle of the oven and bake about 40 minutes until puffed, browned on top and still slightly soft in the centre. Do not open the oven door during cooking!
Serve at once on heated plates.

Calories: 335;
Protein 17 g;
Carbohydrate 13.2 g;
Fibre 2.8 g;
Fat 24.5 g/serving

garlic roast beets

MAKES 4 SERVINGS

4	medium beets, washed and trimmed
8	whole garlic cloves, peeled, sliced
2	Tbsp. [30 mL] extra virgin olive oil
	Grated peel and juice of 1/2 large orange
	Grated peel and juice of 1/2 large lemon
2	Tbsp. [30 mL] minced fresh parsley
2-3	tsp. [10-15 mL] minced fresh thyme
	Coarse black pepper to taste
	Coarse sea salt to taste

*Calories: 100;
Protein 1.2 g;
Carbohydrate 9 g;
Fibre 4.5 g;
Fat 7 g/serving*

1. Preheat oven to 350°F [180°C].

2. Place the beets and garlic cloves in the centre of a square of foil. Fold up the foil around the beets to make a tight seal. Place in the oven to roast for about 1-1/2 hours, or until the beets are tender when pricked with a skewer.

3. Remove package from oven and open foil. Let stand 2-3 minutes while you whisk together all remaining ingredients in a small bowl.

4. Pierce each beet with a fork, holding it over the sink while you scrape off the skins with a knife. [It is possible to peel all 4 beets with no juice getting on either you or the counters!]

5. Mash the soft garlic cloves in the bottom of a large bowl. Slice the beets into the bowl. Toss with dressing and serve at once.

potatoes au gratin
MAKES 8 SERVINGS

1/2	tsp. [3 mL] unsalted butter
1	garlic clove, peeled, halved
1	cup [250 mL] homogenized milk
1	cup [250 mL] crème fraîche*
4	Yukon gold potatoes [about 2 lbs./1 kg], peeled, very thinly sliced**
1/4	tsp. [2 mL] salt
1/8	tsp. [1 mL] freshly ground black pepper
	Freshly grated nutmeg
2	Tbsp. [30 mL] fine dry bread crumbs
1/4	cup [60 mL] grated Gruyère cheese

*See recipe below.
**For best results, slice using a mandolin or a food processor fitted with a metal blade for thin even slices.

1. Preheat oven to 350°F [180°C].
2. Lightly butter the inside of a 9" x 13" [23 x 33 cm] baking dish, then rub with the cut sides of the garlic cloves. Discard garlic.
3. Combine milk and crème fraîche in a large saucepan and whisk over medium heat until hot but not boiling. Remove from the heat.
4. Gently stir in sliced potatoes until they are completely coated. Stir in seasonings.
5. Transfer to prepared baking dish, arranging potato slices in layers. Pour any remaining sauce over top. Scatter with bread crumbs and grated cheese. Bake uncovered in the centre of the preheated oven for 45 minutes or until potatoes are tender when pierced and top is golden.

Crème fraîche: To make crème fraîche, combine 1 cup [250 mL] whipping cream with 2 Tbsp. [30 mL] buttermilk in a glass jar. Cover and set aside at room temperature for 8-24 hours or until very thick. Stir well before covering and refrigerate up to 10 days. It thickens even more once refrigerated. Crème fraîche is excellent for stirring into hot dishes, such as soups, as it won't curdle. Or serve spooned over fresh fruits such as strawberries and peaches. For a lighter Gratin, use 2 cups [500 mL] homogenized milk in place of crème fraîche and sprinkle layers of potatoes with 2 Tbsp. [30 mL] all-purpose flour for thickening before baking.

Calories 259; Protein 6.8 g; Carbohydrate 27.6 g; Fibre 2.3 g; Fat 14 g/serving

PHOTO: PHILIPPE MARTIN-MORICE

swiss chard sautéed with pine nuts

MAKES 6 SERVINGS

1	bunch Swiss chard, red or green
2	tsp. [10 mL] olive oil
1/4	cup [60 mL] pine nuts
2	garlic cloves, finely chopped
2	green onions, finely chopped [optional]
	Juice of 1/2 lemon
	Salt and pepper to taste

Calories: 82;
Protein 2.3 g;
Carbohydrate 4.8 g;
Fibre 2.3 g;
Fat 7.3 g/serving

1. Remove the stems from the Swiss chard. Cut the stems into 1/4"-1/2" [0.6-1.25 cm] pieces. Coarsely chop the leaves. Rinse well but do not dry.

2. In a large non-stick skillet, heat oil over medium heat. Add pine nuts and cook, stirring constantly, for a couple of minutes or until golden. Remove pine nuts from pan and set aside.

3. Add garlic and green onions to skillet; cook on low heat until soft and fragrant [add a bit of water if vegetables start to stick].

4. Add the chard stems and cook until tender, about 2 minutes. Add the chard leaves, stirring constantly; cook until both leaves and stems are tender, about 3-5 minutes.

5. Stir in lemon juice. Season to taste with salt and pepper.

6. Add reserved pine nuts. Cook until heated through.

Note: This recipe can use any type of greens: beet greens, bok choy, spinach, kale, curly endive, Swiss chard or any other combination. The greens can be served as a side dish or under grilled fish or chicken. Don't be surprised by the large amount of greens in this recipe; they reduce considerably when cooked.

broccoli and carrot bake

MAKES 6 SERVINGS

8	cups [2 L] broccoli florets
6	cups [1.5 L] julienned carrots [8 large]
4	cups [1 L] large shallots, peeled, quartered
1	cup [250 mL] dry white wine
2/3	cup [150 mL] Italian-style salad dressing
1	cup [250 mL] homemade whole-wheat bread crumbs
4	Tbsp. [60 mL] melted garlic butter
1/2	tsp. [3 mL] coarse black pepper
1/2	tsp. [3 mL] salt

1. Preheat oven to 450F [230C].

2. Combine broccoli, carrots and shallots in a casserole that is not too deep.

3. Mix together the wine and dressing and pour over top of the vegetables.

4. Combine the crumbs, melted garlic butter, salt and pepper. Spread over top of the vegetables. Cover with lid or foil. Bake in the oven for 15 minutes.

5. Remove cover and bake another 15 minutes or until carrots and broccoli stems are just tender [broccoli should still be bright in colour – do not overcook] and crumb topping is starting to brown.

Note: This dish can be prepared earlier in the day, then covered and baked alongside any roast towards the end of its cooking time.

Calories: 408;
Protein 12 g;
Carbohydrate 62.6 g;
Fibre 11.1 g;
Fat 11 g/serving

[home baking]

169

Raisin Bran Loaf
Banana Chocolate Chip Loaf
Cranberry Orange Loaf
Lemon Poppy Seed Bars
Peanut Butter Fudge Brownies
Viennese Florentines
Multigrain Pumpkin Seed Bread
Blueberry Cornbread Muffins
Apple Breakfast Cookies
Double Chocolate Chip Cookies
Oatmeal Bumbleberry Squares
Lemon Lace Cookies
Christmas Brownies
Double Chocolate Mocha Ice Cream Cookies
Strawberry Muffins with Crunchy Pecan Streusel
Old-Fashioned Cranberry Scones

raisin bran loaf

MAKES 12 SLICES

1	egg, beaten
2	Tbsp. [30 mL] vegetable oil
3/4	cup [175 mL] 1% buttermilk
1/2	cup [125 mL] applesauce
1-3/4	cups [425 mL] all-purpose flour
1	cup [250 mL] packed golden sugar
1/4	tsp. [2 mL] salt
2-1/2	tsp. [13 mL] baking powder
1	tsp. [5 mL] baking soda
1	tsp. [5 mL] cinnamon
3/4	tsp. [4 mL] allspice
3/4	cup [175 mL] all-bran cereal
1	cup [250 mL] dark raisins

Calories: 227;
Protein 4 g;
Carbohydrate 46 g;
Fibre 2.7 g;
Fat 3 g/slice

1. Preheat oven to 350°F [180°C].

2. Spray a Pyrex loaf pan with vegetable cooking spray.

3. Prepare bowl No. 1: Eggs, oil, buttermilk and applesauce.; mix.

4. Prepare bowl No. 2: Flour, sugar, salt, baking powder, baking soda, spices, cereal and raisins; mix.

5. Add bowl No. 1 to bowl No. 2. Mix gently to combine ingredients. Do not completely blend wet and dry; leave slightly lumpy.

6. Transfer batter to prepared pan. Bake about 50-55 minutes or until a toothpick inserted in the centre comes out clean.

7. Let cool in pan 10 minutes. Turn out onto rack to cool completely before wrapping. Slices better the next day.

Fruit for fat: To cut down on both calories and fat in your home baking of items like quick breads (loaves and muffins) without compromising moisture and taste, simply substitute puréed fruit for some or all of the fat in the original recipe. The best substitutes we found are applesauce, mashed banana and puréed prunes. Puréed prunes can get messy, but strained prunes from the baby food section work well.

banana chocolate chip loaf

MAKES 12 SLICES

1	egg, beaten
2	Tbsp. [30 mL] vegetable oil
1/2	cup [125 mL] 2% milk
1	cup [250 mL] mashed banana [about 2 large]
1	tsp. [5 mL] vanilla
2	cups [500 mL] all-purpose flour
1-1/3	cups [325 mL] granulated sugar
1/2	tsp. [3 mL] salt
2	tsp. [10 mL] baking powder
1/2	tsp. [3 mL] baking soda
3/4	cup [175 mL] semi-sweet chocolate chips

1. Preheat oven to 350°F [180°C].

2. Spray a Pyrex loaf pan with vegetable cooking spray.

3. Prepare bowl No. 1: Egg, oil, milk, mashed banana [mashed with a fork on a plate] and vanilla; mix.

4. Prepare bowl No. 2: All remaining ingredients; mix.

5. Add bowl No. 1 to bowl No. 2. Mix gently to combine ingredients. Do not completely blend wet and dry; leave slightly lumpy. Transfer batter to prepared pan.

6. Bake about 60-65 minutes or until a toothpick inserted in the centre comes out clean.

7. Let cool in pan 10 minutes. Turn out onto rack to cool completely before wrapping. Slices better the next day.

Calories: 308;
Protein 4 g;
Carbohydrate 55 g;
Fibre 1 g;
Fat 8 g/slice

cranberry orange loaf

MAKES 12 SLICES

1	egg, beaten
1/4	cup [60 mL] vegetable oil
	Grated peel and juice of 1 orange
2	cups [500 mL] all-purpose flour
1	cup [250 mL] granulated sugar
1/4	tsp. [2 mL] salt
1-1/2	tsp. [8 mL] baking powder
1/2	tsp. [3 mL] baking soda
1/2	cup [125 mL] finely chopped pecans
1	cup [250 mL] frozen or fresh cranberries*
	Skim milk

*Do not thaw frozen cranberries.

*Calories: 253;
Protein 4 g;
Carbohydrate 39 g;
Fibre 1.5 g;
Fat 9 g/slice*

1. Preheat oven to 350°F [180°C].

2. Spray a Pyrex loaf pan with vegetable cooking spray.

3. Prepare bowl No. 1: Egg, oil, orange peel and juice, enough skim milk to make the orange juice up to 1 cup [250 mL] – usually about 2/3 cup [150 mL]; mix.

4. Prepare bowl No. 2: Flour, sugar, salt, baking powder, baking soda, pecans and cranberries; mix.

5. Add bowl No. 1 to bowl No. 2. Mix gently to combine ingredients. Do not completely blend wet and dry; leave slightly lumpy. Transfer batter to prepared pan.

6. Bake about 55-65 minutes or until a toothpick inserted in the centre comes out clean.

7. Let cool in pan 10 minutes. Turn out onto rack to cool completely before wrapping. Slices better the next day.

lemon poppy seed bars

MAKES 24 BARS

Crust:

2	cups [500 mL] all-purpose flour
1/2	cup [125 mL] icing sugar
1	cup [250 mL] unsalted butter [room temperature]

Filling:

4	eggs
3/4	cup [175 mL] granulated sugar
1	Tbsp. [15 mL] all-purpose flour
1	Tbsp. [15 mL] poppy seeds
1	tsp. [5 mL] vanilla
1	Tbsp. [15 mL] grated lemon peel
1/2	cup [125 mL] freshly squeezed lemon juice
1/3	cup [75 mL] buttermilk
2	Tbsp. [30 mL] icing sugar, for dusting

1. To make the crust: Preheat oven to 350°F [180°C]. In a medium-sized bowl, combine flour and icing sugar. Using a pastry blender, cut butter into the flour until the mixture is crumbly and the butter is well incorporated.

2. Spread mixture onto the bottom of a 9" x 13" [23 x 32.5 cm] pan [it will be crumbly] and press down evenly.

3. Bake for 20 minutes or until the pastry base has set and is a light golden brown. Set aside. Do not turn off the oven.

4. To prepare the filling: In a large bowl, whisk eggs and sugar together until well combined. Whisk in the flour, poppy seeds, vanilla, grated lemon peel, lemon juice and buttermilk.

5. Pour filling over pre-baked crust and bake for 25-30 minutes. The bars are done when the filling is set and firm to the touch.

6. Allow the lemon bars to cool. Dust with icing sugar and cut into 24 pieces. Wrap the bars well and store at room temperature.

*Calories: 148;
Protein 2 g ;
Carbohydrate 8 g;
Fibre 0.3 g;
Fat 18 g/bar*

peanut butter fudge brownies

MAKES 16 BARS

Brownie:
1/3	cup [75 mL] unsweetened chocolate pieces
1/2	cup [125 mL] unsalted butter [room temperature]
1/2	cup [125 mL] granulated sugar
1/4	cup [60 mL] lightly packed brown sugar
2	tsp. [10 mL] vanilla
3	eggs
2/3	cup [150 mL] all-purpose flour
1/2	tsp. [3 mL] baking powder
1/2	tsp. [3 mL] salt
1/2	cup [125 mL] crunchy natural peanut butter

Icing:
1/2	cup [125 mL] cream cheese [room temperature]
1/4	cup [60 mL] unsalted butter [room temperature]
1/3	cup [75 mL] crunchy natural peanut butter
1/2	cup [125 mL] icing sugar

Calories: 278;
Protein 6 g;
Carbohydrate 21 g;
Fibre 1 g;
Fat 20 g/bar

1. Preheat the oven to 350°F [180°C] and lightly butter or spray an 8" [20 cm] square baking dish or cake pan.

2. Melt unsweetened chocolate pieces and set aside to cool.

3. In a large bowl, combine butter, both sugars and vanilla. Using an electric mixer, beat until light and fluffy; add the eggs, one at a time, beating well after each addition.

4. Combine flour, baking powder and salt; add to batter; mix just to combine.

5. Transfer half of the batter to another bowl; add the melted and cooled chocolate. Stir well to combine.

6. Add the peanut butter to the remaining batter and stir well to combine. Transfer the peanut butter mixture to the pan, spreading it evenly over the bottom of the pan.

7. Spread the chocolate batter over the peanut butter batter to form an even layer.

8. Bake approximately 30-35 minutes or until a toothpick inserted into the centre comes out with dry crumbs on it.

9. Allow to cool completely before frosting with the cream cheese icing.

10. Make the icing: In a medium-sized bowl, use an electric mixer to cream together cream cheese and butter until well combined. Add peanut butter and icing sugar and beat until fluffy.

11. Once cooled, frost with the icing; chill until the icing has set, about 1 hour.

12. Cut the brownies into 16 squares and store well wrapped, in the refrigerator until serving time.

viennese florentines

MAKES ABOUT 24 COOKIES

3/4	cup [175 mL] finely chopped blanched almonds
3/4	cup [175 mL] finely chopped mixed peel
1/4	cup [60 mL] finely chopped glacé cherries
1/2	cup [125 mL] all-purpose flour
	Grated peel and juice of 1 large lemon
3	Tbsp. [45 mL] butter
1/3	cup [75 mL] packed golden sugar
1	Tbsp. [15 mL] corn syrup
6	squares semi-sweet chocolate

1. Preheat oven to 350°F [180°C].

2. Combine first 4 ingredients and mix well. Add grated peel.

3. In a small saucepan combine juice, butter, sugar and syrup. Heat until bubbly. Add to dry ingredients; mix well to totally combine. Work quickly at this point to make sure the mixture does not cool completely.

4. Drop in small mounds [about 2 tsp./10 mL each] on a lightly greased or sprayed [or non-stick] cookie sheet. Leave lots of room between the cookies. [You should put about 6 cookies on each sheet.]

5. Dipping a drinking glass bottom in cold water in between, flatten each mound until very thin. Bake about 6 minutes. Watch that they do not burn!

6. Let cool about 10 minutes on the pan; remove to a rack upside down to cool completely.

7. When totally cool [and very crisp], melt the chocolate in the microwave or on the stove. Paint the flat bottoms of the cookies [which should now be facing up on the rack] with the chocolate; pull a baker's rake across each to make wiggly lines in the chocolate. Or use the tines of a fork to make the traditional lines. Let set [in a warm kitchen you may have to refrigerate briefly] before serving.

Note: These cookies should be extremely crisp – to keep crisp, store in an airtight tin.

Calories: 139;
Protein 1 g;
Carbohydrate 18 g;
Fibre 0.9 g;
Fat 7 g/cookie

multigrain pumpkin seed bread

MAKES 2 LOAVES [32 SLICES]

4	eggs
2-1/4	cups [560 mL] granulated sugar
1	cup [250 mL] vegetable oil
1	[14 fl. oz./398 mL] tin pure pumpkin
2	cups [500 mL] all-purpose flour
1	cup [250 mL] 100% all-purpose whole-wheat flour
1	Tbsp. [15 mL] baking powder
2	tsp. [10 mL] baking soda
2	tsp. [10 mL] ground cinnamon
1/2	tsp. [2 mL] each ground cloves, ground nutmeg and salt
	Finely grated peel of 1 orange
1	cup [250 mL] seedless golden raisins
1/2	cup [125 mL] unsalted sunflower seeds, toasted
1/2	cup [125 mL] unsalted pumpkin seeds, toasted
1/3	cup [75 mL] dark flaxseed

Calories: 189;
Protein 2.4 g;
Carbohydrate 24.5 g;
Fibre 1.5 g;
Fat 9.8 g/slice

1. Preheat oven to 350°F [180°C]. Grease two 9" x 5" x 3" [23 x 12 x 8 cm] loaf pans and set aside.

2. Combine eggs, sugar and vegetable oil in a large mixing bowl. Whisk together until evenly blended. Whisk in pumpkin.

3. In a separate bowl combine flours, baking powder, soda, seasonings and orange peel. Stir to blend. Gradually stir into pumpkin mixture. Do not over-beat.

4. Fold in remaining ingredients.

5. Divide batter equally between prepared pans. Smooth the tops and tap pans gently once on counter to remove any air pockets.

6. Bake about 60-70 minutes, or until a cake tester inserted into the centre comes out clean. Transfer pans to racks and cool for 10 minutes. Then turn out cakes onto racks and cool completely.

7. Wrap in plastic wrap and store at room temperature for up to 2 days or over-wrap with foil and plastic wrap and freeze for up to 1 month.

multigrain
pumpkin
seed
bread

blueberry
cornbread
muffins

PHOTO: JOE BORRELLI

blueberry cornbread muffins

MAKES 12 MUFFINS

1	cup [250 mL]	yellow cornmeal
3	cups [750 mL]	all-purpose flour
3/4	cup [175 mL]	granulated sugar
2	Tbsp. [30 mL]	baking powder
1/2	tsp. [3 mL]	salt
1-1/2	cups [375 mL]	2% milk
1	cup [250 mL]	butter, melted
2		eggs, slightly beaten
1	cup [250 mL]	blueberries, fresh or frozen

1. Preheat oven to 350°F [180°C]. Line a large 12-cup muffin tin with paper muffin cups.

2. Combine dry ingredients in a large bowl.

3. Mix together milk, butter and beaten eggs and add to flour mixture all at once. Mix until just combined.

4. Gently fold in blueberries.

5. Fill muffin cups with batter and bake on the centre rack of the oven for about 30 minutes or until tops are crisp and a toothpick comes out clean when inserted into the centre of a muffin. Turn muffins out of tin and let cool on a wire rack.

Calories: 375;
Protein 6.5 g;
Carbohydrate 49 g;
Fibre 2 g;
Fat 17 g/serving

apple breakfast cookies

MAKES 16 LARGE COOKIES

3	tart apples, cored, peeled and grated*
1-1/2	cups [375 mL] 9-grain cereal blend**
1/2	cup [125 mL] dried cranberries
1/2	cup [125 mL] chopped dried apples
1/2	cup [125 mL] raisins or chopped dates
1/2	cup [125 mL] apple juice
1/3	cup [75 mL] molasses or corn syrup
1	egg
1	egg white
1/2	cup [125 mL] packed brown sugar
1/4	cup [60 mL] canola oil
2	tsp. [10 mL] vanilla
1/2	cup [125 mL] all-purpose flour
1/2	tsp. [3 mL] salt
1	tsp. [5 mL] cinnamon
1/4	tsp. [2 mL] each ground cardamom and nutmeg
1/4	tsp. [2 mL] baking soda

*Use a large-holed grater.
**We used Roger's brand.

Calories: 159;
Protein 2 g;
Carbohydrate 30 g;
Fibre 1.6 g;
Fat 4 g/cookie

1. Preheat oven to 350°F [180°C]. Line 2 baking sheets with parchment paper.

2. Combine first 7 ingredients in a large bowl; mix well. Let stand 10 minutes to soften the grains and dried fruit.

3. In a small bowl, whisk together egg, egg white, sugar, oil and vanilla. Pour into fruit mixture; mix well.

4. Blend together flour, salt, spices and soda. Fold into fruit mixture; let stand another 10 minutes.

5. Using a 1/4 cup [60 mL] measure, scoop batter onto parchment-lined baking sheets, spacing 2" [5 cm] apart.

6. Bake 8 minutes; rotate trays and bake another 8 minutes. Remove from oven; transfer cookies to cooling racks.

7. When cooled, store in an airtight tin between layers of wax paper. The cookies keep well for 4-6 days. Freeze for longer storage.

double chocolate chip cookies

MAKES 30 COOKIES

1/2	cup [125 mL] soft butter or margarine
3	squares semi-sweet chocolate, melted
1-1/2	cups [375 mL] packed brown sugar
2	eggs
2	cups [500 mL] all-purpose flour
1	tsp. [5 mL] baking powder
1/2	cup [125 mL] finely chopped walnuts
1/2	[300 g] pkg. semi-sweet chocolate chips
1/2	[300 g] pkg. butterscotch* chips

*All semi-sweet chocolate chips can be used in place of half butterscotch ones if you prefer.

---

1. Preheat oven to 375°F [190°C].

2. Combine butter and melted chocolate in a large bowl. Use an electric mixer to beat together with the brown sugar. Beat in eggs, one at a time.

3. Combine all remaining dry ingredients in a medium-sized bowl; mix well. Add to bowl. Use a wooden spoon to mix batter together completely.

4. Drop batter from a tablespoon onto ungreased cookie sheets – about 12 to a sheet. Bake for about 10 minutes.

5. Let cool on pan 5 minutes before transferring to a rack to cool completely.

Calories: 181;
Protein 2.4 g;
Carbohydrate 25 g;
Fibre 0.4 g;
Fat 9.1 g/cookie

oatmeal bumbleberry squares

MAKES 20 SQUARES

Base:

1/2	cup [125 mL]	soft butter or margarine
1/3	cup [75 mL]	granulated sugar
1		egg, lightly beaten
1	cup [250 mL]	all-purpose flour
1/2	cup [125 mL]	instant oats

Filling:

1	cup [250 mL]	well-drained thawed frozen raspberries
3/4	cup [175 mL]	well-drained frozen blueberries
1/4	cup [60 mL]	dried cranberries
1/3	cup [75 mL]	granulated sugar

Topping:

2		egg whites*
1	tsp. [5 mL]	vanilla
1/2	cup [125 mL]	packed brown sugar
1/2	cup [125 mL]	finely chopped walnuts

Or use liquid egg white (available in the dairy department).

Calories: 161;
Protein 2.9 g;
Carbohydrate 23 g;
Fibre 1.1 g;
Fat 7 g/square

1. Preheat oven to 325°F [160°C]. Spray or lightly grease and flour a 9" [23 cm] square cake pan.

2. Use an electric mixer to cream the soft butter and sugar together for the base. Beat in the egg, flour and instant oats. Press firmly and evenly into the bottom of the prepared pan. Bake about 15 to 20 minutes. Let cool.

3. Combine the well-drained fruit [fresh fruit can be substituted in season] and sugar. Spread over the cooled base.

4. Increase oven temperature to 375°F [190°C].

5. Combine egg whites and vanilla in a medium bowl. Using an electric mixer, beat until nearly stiff; add brown sugar while continuing to beat until you have a stiff meringue. Fold in nuts. Spread over fruit.

6. Bake about 25 minutes. Cool completely before cutting into squares.

Note: This square works nicely as a dessert – it's easier to eat with a fork than with your fingers!

PHOTO: JOE BORRELLI

lemon lace cookies

MAKES 24 COOKIES

1	cup [250 mL] all-purpose flour, sifted
1/4	tsp. [2 mL] salt
1	cup [250 mL] finely chopped blanched almonds
3/4	cup [175 mL] packed golden sugar
1/2	cup [125 mL] light corn syrup
1/4	cup [60 mL] unsalted butter
1	tsp. [5 mL] lemon extract
	Finely grated peel of 2 lemons
1	Tbsp. [15 mL] fresh lemon juice

1. Preheat oven to 350°F [180°C]. Lightly butter or spray a heavy baking sheet.

2. In a large bowl, stir together flour, salt and almonds.

3. In a saucepan, combine sugar, corn syrup and butter; bring to a boil over moderate heat. Remove from heat and stir in the flour mixture, lemon extract, lemon peel and juice.

4. Drop 1/2 tsp. [3 mL] batter, about 2" [5 cm] apart, onto the prepared baking sheet. Bake 8-10 minutes or until lightly browned at the edges.

5. Let cookies cool on baking sheet for a few minutes before transferring to a wire rack to cool completely. To create curled cookies, wrap warm cookies immediately around a rolling pin to cool.

Calories: 120;
Protein 1.8 g;
Carbohydrate 17.5 g;
Fibre 0.7 g;
Fat 5.3 g/cookie

christmas brownies

MAKES 16 BROWNIES

1	cup [250 mL] all-purpose flour
1/4	tsp. [2 mL] salt
1/2	cup [125 mL] finely chopped walnuts [optional]
1	cup [250 mL] jumbo semi-sweet chocolate chips
1/2	cup [125 mL] soft butter or margarine
1	cup [250 mL] granulated sugar
2	eggs
1/2	cup [125 mL] mincemeat
2	squares semi-sweet chocolate, melted
1	tsp. [5 mL] vanilla

Topping:

2	cups [500 mL] miniature marshmallows
2	squares semi-sweet chocolate, melted

*Calories: 293;
Protein 4.0 g;
Carbohydrate 39 g;
Fibre 0.4 g;
Fat 16 g/brownie*

1. Preheat oven to 350°F [180°C]. Spray or grease and flour a 9" [23 cm] square cake pan.
2. Combine first 4 ingredients in a bowl; mix well.
3. In a large bowl, combine butter or margarine and sugar. Cream together until fluffy, using an electric mixer at high speed. Beat in eggs, one at a time. Beat in mincemeat, melted chocolate and vanilla. Beat in dry ingredient mix.
4. Spread batter evenly in prepared pan.
5. Bake in the centre of the oven for about 40-45 minutes or until a toothpick inserted in the centre comes out clean.
6. Cool 15 minutes in pan. Spread marshmallows evenly over top of warm brownie in pan. Place under preheated broiler 5"-6" [12.5-15 cm] from the heat. Watch carefully and broil only until golden brown.
7. Melt remaining 2 squares of semi-sweet chocolate with 2 Tbsp. [30 mL] of milk and drizzle over top of the warm marshmallows.
8. Cool to just warm or room temperature before cutting into squares and serving.

double chocolate mocha ice cream cookies

MAKES 24 TO 36 COOKIES

1	cup [250 mL] butter
1	cup [250 mL] packed brown sugar
1/4	cup [60 mL] granulated sugar
2	eggs
1	tsp. [5 mL] baking soda
1/4	tsp. [2 mL] salt
2-1/2	Tbsp. instant coffee [38 mL] dissolved in 1 Tbsp. [15 mL] hot water
2	cups [500 mL] all-purpose flour
1/2	cup [125 mL] cocoa powder, sifted
3/4	cup [185 mL] chocolate chips
4	cups [1 L] coffee or espresso-flavoured ice cream

1. Preheat oven to 350°F [180°C].

2. In a mixing bowl, cream butter using an electric mixer until light and fluffy. Add both sugars and eggs. Mix together, scraping sides and bottom of bowl.

3. Add baking soda, salt and coffee and mix until combined.

4. Stir in flour and sifted cocoa powder just until combined.

5. Stir in chocolate chips just until combined.

6. Let cookie dough chill in refrigerator for 20-30 minutes.

7. Drop tablespoonfuls of cookie dough onto a parchment paper-lined baking sheet. Shape dough into balls. For smaller cookies, press down gently with fingers. For larger cookies, gently press dough with the palm of your hand.

8. Bake in preheated oven for 10-12 minutes, just until edges of cookies are set.

9. Remove from oven and let cool on baking sheet for a few minutes before transferring to a cooling rack.

10. Allow cookies to cool completely before using.

11. Remove coffee-flavoured ice cream from the freezer. Let thaw for 5 minutes. Scoop desired amount of ice cream onto the bottom side of one cookie. Spread with a knife or spatula to flatten slightly.

12. Top with the second cookie, flat side down. Gently press to sandwich cookies together. If desired, scoop ice cream into a 1/4 or 1/2 cup [60 or 125 mL] measuring cup. Pack tightly. Unmould ice cream onto cookie. This will produce an even, rounded serving of ice cream in each sandwich.

13. Serve filled cookies immediately or wrap each in plastic wrap and place in the freezer. If you are not planning to serve them right away, store wrapped cookies in a plastic container in the freezer. Frozen cookies will keep for up to 2 weeks.

*Calories: 339;
Protein 4.3 g;
Carbohydrate 40 g;
Fibre 1.6 g;
Fat 19.6 g/cookie*

strawberry muffins with crunchy pecan streusel

MAKES 12 MUFFINS

Streusel:

1/2	cup [125 mL] all-purpose flour
1/3	cup [75 mL] packed brown sugar
6	Tbsp. [90 mL] butter, cubed, lightly chilled
1/3	cup [75 mL] pecans, coarsely chopped

Muffins:

1/2	cup [125 mL] unsalted butter, melted, cooled
1/2	cup [125 mL] firmly packed brown sugar
1/4	cup [60 mL] granulated sugar
1	egg
2	tsp. [10 mL] vanilla
1	cup [250 mL] buttermilk
2	cups [500 mL] all-purpose flour
1/2	cup [125 mL] wheat germ
1/2	tsp. [3 mL] salt
1	Tbsp. [15 mL] baking powder
1	tsp. [5 mL] baking soda
1-1/2	cups [375 mL] strawberries, cleaned, hulled

Calories: 308;
Protein 4.25 g;
Carbohydrate 36.5 g;
Fibre 2.2 g;
Fat 16.7 g/muffin

1. Preheat oven to 375°F [190°C]. Line 12 muffin cups with paper liners or lightly spray with cooking spray. Set aside.

2. To make the streusel: In a medium bowl, combine the flour and brown sugar. Using a pastry blender or your fingertips, work in the butter until the mixture begins to hold together and look crumbly. Add the pecans and set aside.

3. To make the muffins: In a large bowl combine the melted butter, both sugars, egg, vanilla extract and buttermilk. Whisk together until well combined. In a large bowl, stir together flour, wheat germ, salt, baking powder and baking soda. Add dry ingredients to the wet ingredients and stir just to combine. Do not over-mix.

4. Slice the strawberries and gently fold them into the batter. Divide the batter between the muffin cups and sprinkle with the streusel topping.

5. Bake for approximately 25-30 minutes, or until the muffins spring back when lightly pressed. Allow to cool for 5 minutes before removing muffins from the pan.

old-fashioned cranberry scones

MAKES 16 SCONES

3	cups [750 mL] all-purpose flour
1/2	tsp. [3 mL] salt
4	tsp. [20 mL] baking powder
1/2	tsp. [3 mL] baking soda
1/2	cup [125 mL] granulated sugar
1/4	cup [60 mL] cold butter
1	cup [250 mL] fresh/frozen cranberries*
10	Tbsp. [150 mL] applesauce
1	[175 g] tub 1-2% plain yogurt
	Grated peel of 1 large orange

Do not thaw if using frozen cranberries.

1. Preheat oven to 425°F [220°C].
2. Combine first 5 ingredients in a large bowl; mix well. Using a pastry blender or 2 knives, cut in butter to the size of peas. Add cranberries; mix well.
3. In a small bowl, combine applesauce, yogurt and peel.
4. Add to dry ingredients bowl; mix gently, with your hands, making sure you leave the dough only just combined – do not knead.
5. Remove dough from bowl to a floured board. Divide in half. Use your hands to gently pat each half into a circle about 8" [20 cm] in diameter. Cut each circle into 8 wedges.
6. Place on a cookie sheet, making sure that scones do not touch each other. Bake about 18-25 minutes or until browned. Cool on a rack.

Calories: 151;
Protein 3 g;
Carbohydrate 27 g;
Fibre 1.2 g;
Fat 3.3 g/scone

[desserts]

Free-Form Fruit Galette
Rhubarb and Orange Pie
Blueberry Lemon Tart
Mile High Peach Pie
Margarita Chiffon Pie
Strawberry Shortcake
Apple, Pear and Cranberry Crisp
Vanilla Bean Butter Cake
Classic Pavlova
Tiramisu
Pumpkin Cheesecake
Summer Strawberry Mousse Cake
Heirloom Chocolate Cake
Mango Pudding
Three Citrus Mousse
Coconut Crème Brûlée
Three Tiered Chocolate Mousse
Iced Strawberry Swirl Soufflé
Cantaloupe Sorbet

free-form fruit galette

MAKES 6 SERVINGS

Pastry:

1-1/4	cups [310 mL] all-purpose flour
1	Tbsp. [15 mL] granulated sugar
1	tsp. [5 mL] grated lemon peel
10	Tbsp. [150 mL] unsalted butter, chilled and cubed
1	tsp. [5 mL] vanilla extract
2	Tbsp. [30 mL] water
	Pinch of salt

Filling:

2-1/2	cups [625 mL] mixed sliced peaches, plums, apricots, raspberries, blueberries, strawberries
1-1/2	Tbsp. [25 mL] all-purpose flour
1/3-1/2	cup [75-125 mL] granulated sugar, to taste

Calories: 365;
Protein 3.8 g;
Carbohydrate 44.7 g;
Fibre 3.5 g;
Fat 19.8 g/serving

1. To make pastry: In a large bowl, combine flour, sugar, lemon peel, salt and butter. Using a pastry blender, cut butter into flour until it resembles coarse crumbs.

2. Combine vanilla and water; gradually add to pastry, using your hands to gently pull the dough together into a ball. Add more water if the pastry is too dry; wrap in waxed paper and refrigerate for 1 hour.

3. Preheat oven to 425°F [210°C].

4. To make filling: Combine prepared fruits in a large bowl and toss with flour; mix in sugar. Set aside.

5. Lightly grease a large, heavy cookie sheet.

6. Remove pastry from refrigerator and roll out dough between sheets of floured waxed paper into a 14" [35 cm] circle. Remove top sheet of waxed paper; invert dough onto prepared cookie sheet. Peel off the waxed paper.

7. Mound the fruit [along with any clinging sugar and flour] into the centre of the pastry. Spread fruit to within 4" [10 cm] of the outside rim. Bring pastry edges up over the fruit, folding the pastry into pleats as necessary to make an approximate 9" [23 cm] free-form shape.

8. Lightly sprinkle pastry with sugar; bake 10 minutes.

9. Reduce heat to 400°F [200°C]; continue baking 35 to 40 minutes, or until fruit is bubbling with juices and crust is golden brown. Allow galette to cool 1/2 hour before carefully removing it to a serving platter.

10. Using a sharp unserrated knife, slice galette into wedges; serve with ice cream.

rhubarb and orange pie

MAKES 6 SERVINGS

Pastry for a 9" [23 cm] single-crust pie

Filling:

4	cups [1 L] cut-up fresh rhubarb*
3	large oranges, peeled, segmented, chopped
1	Tbsp. [15 mL] fresh lemon juice
1/2	cup [125 mL] Seville orange marmalade
4	Tbsp. [60 mL] all-purpose flour
3/4	cup [175 mL] packed golden sugar
3/4	tsp. [4 mL] ground ginger

Topping:

1/2	cup [125 mL] very soft butter or margarine
1/4	cup [60 mL] ground pecans or hazelnuts
3/4	cup [175 mL] quick oats
3/4	cup [175 mL] all-purpose flour
1/2	cup [125 mL] packed golden sugar
1/2	tsp. [3 mL] ground ginger
	Pinch nutmeg

If you are using 4 cups [1 L] frozen rhubarb chunks, do not thaw and use slightly more flour.

1. Preheat oven to 400° F [200°C].
2. Roll out pastry on a floured board to a circle slightly larger than a 9" [23 cm] deep-dish pie plate. Fit into the plate, pushing sides and bottom in firmly without stretching. Fold under the overhang and flute attractively. Refrigerate while you make the filling and topping.
3. To make the filling, combine rhubarb, oranges, lemon juice and marmalade in a large bowl and mix well.
4. Mix together the flour, sugar and ginger. Toss the rhubarb mixture with the flour mixture in the large bowl.
5. In a smaller bowl, combine all the topping ingredients and mix or rub together with your fingers until you have a rough, crumb-like texture.
6. Pile rhubarb filling into the prepared crust. Spread the crumb topping over top.
7. Place on a baking sheet and bake about 20 minutes. Reduce heat to 375°F [190°C] and continue baking another 35-40 minutes.
8. Let cool completely before cutting.

Calories: 740;
Protein 9.2 g;
Carbohydrate 118 g;
Fibre 5.9 g;
Fat 28 g/serving

PHOTO: JOE BORRELLI

blueberry lemon tart

MAKES 8 SERVINGS

Pastry for a 9" [23 cm] fluted flan pan with removable bottom*
3/4 cup [175 mL] lemon curd [or "lemon cheese"]**

Filling:

1	cup [250 mL] sour cream
3/4	cup [175 mL] granulated sugar
2	Tbsp. [30 mL] all-purpose flour
1/4	tsp. [2 mL] salt
1	tsp. [5 mL] almond extract
1	tsp. [5 mL] grated lemon peel
1	egg
2-1/2	cups [625 mL] fresh blueberries

Topping:

3	Tbsp. [45 mL] instant oatmeal
3	Tbsp. [45 mL] medium unsweetened coconut
1	Tbsp. [15 mL] melted butter or margarine

*Make sure the pastry has been refrigerated at least 1 hour before rolling it out to fit into the flan pan.
**Lemon spread or prepared lemon pie filling can be substituted.

Calories: 371;
Protein 4.5 g;
Carbohydrate 49 g;
Fibre 3 g;
Fat 18 g/serving

1. Preheat oven to 400°F [200°C].

2. Prepare the filling by beating together all the ingredients [except the blueberries] in a bowl for 2 minutes, using an electric mixer. Fold in the blueberries.

3. Spread the lemon curd over the pastry in the flan pan. Spread the filling over top, distributing the berries evenly.

4. Bake for 25 minutes.

5. Mix topping ingredients together with a fork. Sprinkle evenly over top surface of the tart; continue baking for a further 10 minutes until golden.

6. Cool on a rack. Chill tart in refrigerator before cutting in slices to serve.

mile high peach pie

MAKES 8 SERVINGS

Crust:

2-1/3	cups [575 mL] all-purpose flour
1	Tbsp. [15 mL] granulated sugar
1/4	tsp. [2 mL] salt
3/4	cup [175 mL] chilled lard, cubed
1/4	cup [60 mL] unsalted butter, chilled, cubed
1/3	cup [75 mL] ice-cold water
1	tsp. [5 mL] white vinegar, chilled

Filling:

1/2	cup [125 mL] granulated sugar
3	Tbsp. [45 mL] cornstarch
2	Tbsp. [30 mL] diced crystallized ginger
1/2	tsp. [3 mL] ground cinnamon
1/8	tsp. [1 mL] fresh grated nutmeg
6	cups [1.5 L] peeled, sliced fresh peaches
1	[125 g] pkg. light cream cheese, cut into small pieces [optional]
1	Tbsp. [15 mL] 1% milk
1	tsp. [5 mL] granulated sugar

---

1. To make crust: Be sure all utensils are chilled, e.g., bowl, forks, ingredients.

2. Combine flour, sugar and salt in a food processor; pulse briefly to mix.

3. Add lard and butter; quickly pulse with an on-and-off motion just until mixture forms large pea-shaped pieces or moist clumps. Transfer to a chilled bowl.

4. Using a fork, lightly stir in water and vinegar just until dough appears to stick together.

5. Gather dough together using your hands. Form dough into a ball and then divide into 2 equal portions and press each into a disk. Wrap in plastic wrap and refrigerate as you prepare the remaining portion of the pie. Dough can be left refrigerated for up to 2 days.

6. To make pie filling, combine 1/2 cup [125 mL] granulated sugar, cornstarch, ginger, cinnamon and nutmeg in a large bowl. Stir to blend. Add sliced peaches and toss to mix well. Gently fold in cream cheese if using.

7. Preheat oven to 425°F [220°C].

8. Roll out 1 disk of dough on a floured surface to a 13" [32.5 cm] round and transfer to a 9" [23 cm] deep-dish pie plate. Transfer peach filling to crust, mounding in the centre.

9. Roll out second disk into a round. Roll up dough onto rolling pin and unroll over top of peaches. Trim leaving a 3/4" [2 cm] overhang. Fold overhang under bottom crust rim and seal by fluting the edge. Brush top of pastry with milk and sprinkle with granulated sugar. Cut 6 slits in top crust to allow steam to escape.

10. Bake in the centre of the oven for 15 minutes. Reduce heat to 350°F [180°C]; bake for 50 minutes to 1 hour longer. Pastry should be golden and filling bubbling. Cool pie for an hour or two before serving.

Calories: 547;
Protein 6.6 g;
Carbohydrate 68.3 g;
Fibre 3 g;
Fat 28.5 g/serving

margarita chiffon pie

MAKES 6 SERVINGS

Crust:

1	cup [250 mL] graham cracker crumbs
3/4	cup [175 mL] finely chopped toasted pecans*
2	Tbsp. [30 mL] packed golden sugar
1/3	cup [75 mL] melted butter
	Generous shaking of nutmeg

Filling:

1	[250 mL] tin frozen margarita mix, thawed
1/2	cup [125 mL] Tequila
1/4	cup [60 mL] Triple Sec [or other orange liqueur]
1-1/2	envelopes unflavoured gelatin
3	eggs, separated
1	cup [250 mL] whipping cream
3	Tbsp. [45 mL] granulated sugar
1	Tbsp. [15 mL] grated lime peel

*Toast the nuts by spreading on a baking sheet and baking in a 350°F [180°C] oven for about 5-8 minutes.

Calories: 690;
Protein 9 g;
Carbohydrate 69.5 g;
Fibre 1.6 g;
Fat 36 g/serving

1. Preheat oven to 350°F [180°C].

2. Combine all crust ingredients and mix well.

3. Press firmly into the bottom and sides of a 9" [23 cm] tart pan [one with a removable bottom is best]. Place on a baking sheet and bake for about 10 minutes. Let cool completely.

4. To make the filling, combine the thawed margarita mix, Tequila, Triple Sec and unflavoured gelatin in a small saucepan. Place over medium heat and stir until heated through and the gelatin has dissolved. Do not boil.

5. Place egg yolks in a small bowl and beat until frothy and turning pale. Off the heat, beat in a little of the gelatin mixture and return both gelatin mixture and yolks to the saucepan. Continue to cook over medium heat, stirring often. Do not boil.

6. When mixture starts to thicken, remove from heat and chill until thickened and quite cold.

7. When the mixture has thickened, beat the egg whites in a small bowl. Then beat the whipping cream in a large bowl, beating in the granulated sugar at the end. Add gelatin mixture and egg whites to the whipped cream; gently fold the three mixtures together. Pile into the baked crust.

8. Place in the refrigerator for at least 4 hours to fully set. If desired, decorate with whirls of sweetened whipped cream and fresh lime twists or shaved chocolate.

strawberry shortcake

MAKES 8 SERVINGS

2	cups [500 mL] all-purpose flour
1/2	tsp. [3 mL] salt
1	Tbsp. [15 mL] baking powder
2	Tbsp. [30 mL] granulated sugar
	Grated peel of 1 lemon
4	Tbsp. [60 mL] cold butter
3/4	cup [175 mL] skim milk
1	cup [250 mL] whipping cream
1	cup [250 mL] no-fat sour cream
4	Tbsp. [60 mL] packed golden sugar, divided
3	cups [750 mL] sliced strawberries

1. Preheat oven to 425°F [220°C].
2. Combine first 5 ingredients in a medium bowl; mix well. Add cold butter; cut in using two knives or a pastry blender until the size of large peas. Add milk, mixing lightly with a fork.
3. Use your hands to gently pull dough together into a ball. Do not squeeze or massage the dough. [You may need 1-2 Tbsp./15-30 mL more or less of milk depending on the heat of your hands and the temperature of the butter. The dough should be soft, with all dry ingredients incorporated.]
4. Place the dough on the counter and gently press into a circle about 7" [17.5 cm] in diameter. Use a sharp knife to cut across the circle four times to make 8 wedges. Place wedges on an ungreased cookie sheet. Bake about 10 minutes or until nicely browned; cool on rack.
5. Place whipping cream in a small bowl; place no-fat sour cream in another small bowl. Use an electric mixer to beat the cream until stiff, beating in 2 Tbsp. [30 mL] of the golden sugar at the last minute. Use a spoon to beat the remaining golden sugar into the no-fat sour cream.
6. Combine cream and sour cream mixtures; mix gently. Slice open each shortcake wedge horizontally. Place bottoms on a serving platter. Dollop the cream mixture onto the bottoms using about 80 per cent of the mixture divided among the 8 pieces. [Yes, it does overflow!]
7. Top with lots of sliced strawberries [reserve 8 pieces for decorating]. Place the shortcake tops on each wedge. Place a small dollop of cream mixture on top of each wedge and top with a piece of strawberry. Serve at once.

Calories: 335;
Protein 8 g;
Carbohydrate 42 g;
Fibre 1.9 g;
Fat 15 g/serving

apple, pear and cranberry crisp

MAKES 6 TO 8 SERVINGS

3/4	cup [175 mL] plus 1 Tbsp. [15 mL] all-purpose flour
3/4	cup [175 mL] plus 1 Tbsp. [15 mL] packed brown sugar
1/2	cup [125 mL] rolled oats
1/2	cup [125 mL] cold butter
3	apples, cored, peeled, sliced
2	pears, cored, peeled, sliced
1/2	cup [125 mL] frozen cranberries

Calories: 362;
Protein 3.7 g;
Carbohydrate 57 g;
Fibre 4.2 g;
Fat 14.4 g/serving

1. Preheat oven to 400°F [200°C].

2. In mixing bowl, combine 3/4 cup [175 mL] flour, 3/4 cup [175 mL] sugar and rolled oats.

3. Cut in butter until mixture resembles coarse meal.

4. Lightly butter a baking dish. Place apples, pears and cranberries in dish and toss with remaining flour and sugar. Top with the oat mixture.

5. Bake for 30-35 minutes or until topping is golden and fruit is tender. Let stand for 5 minutes before serving.

apple
pear
cranberry
crisp

PHOTO: JOE BORRELLI

vanilla bean butter cake

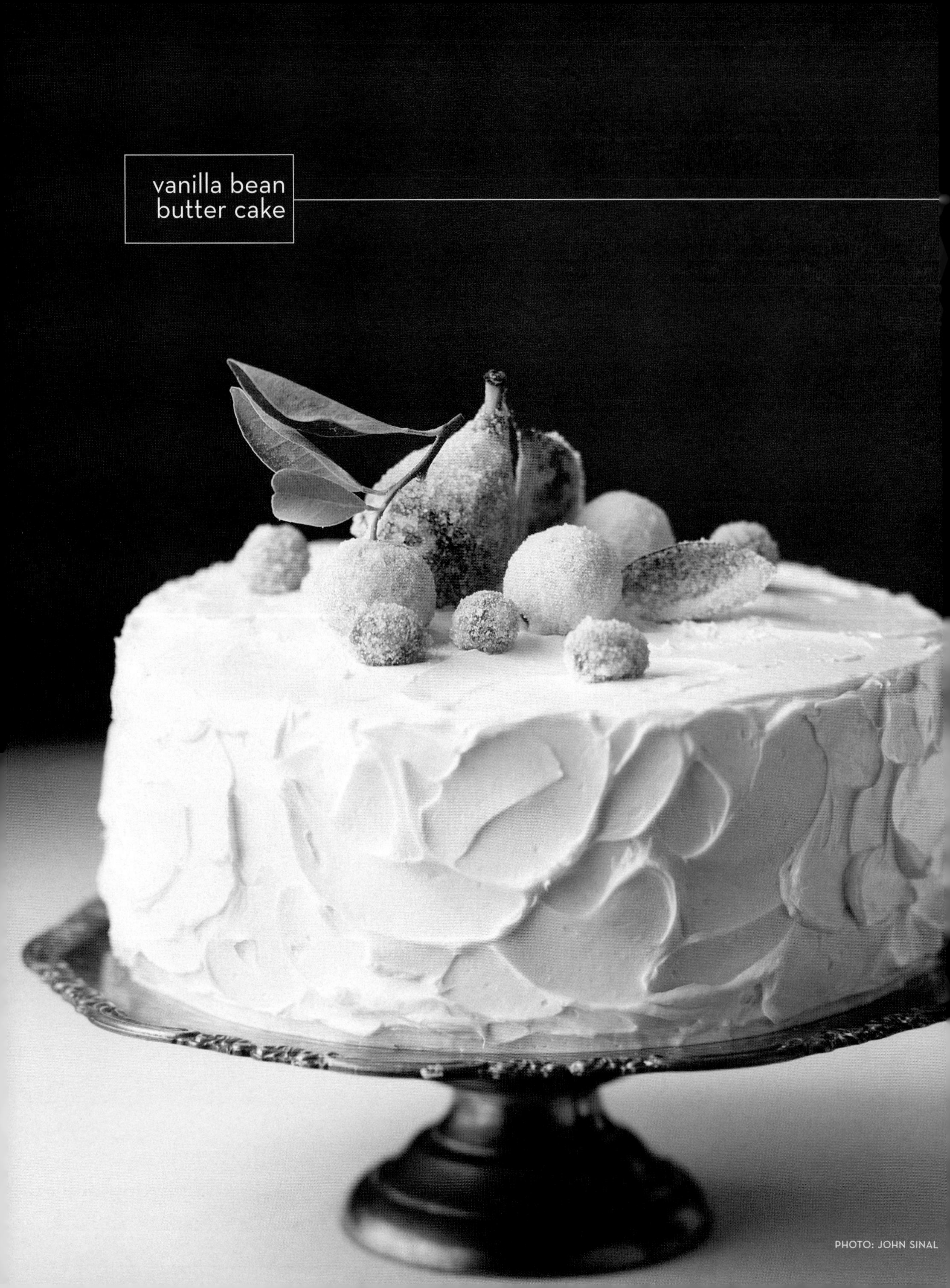

PHOTO: JOHN SINAL

vanilla bean butter cake
with cranberry curd and butter icing
MAKES 12 SERVINGS

Cake:

1	cup [250 mL] 2% milk
3	eggs
1	Tbsp. [15 mL] vanilla
3	cups [750 mL] cake flour, sifted
1-1/2	cups [750 mL] granulated sugar
4	tsp. [20 mL] baking powder
1	tsp. [5 mL] salt
3/4	cup [175 mL] unsalted butter, softened
	Seed scrapings from 1 plump vanilla bean [optional]

Cranberry Curd:

2-1/2	cups [625 mL] cranberries [thawed if frozen]
1/2	cup [125 mL] water
4	Tbsp. [60 mL] unsalted butter
3/4	cup [175 mL] granulated sugar
3	eggs [room temperature]

Butter Icing:

2	cups [500 mL] unsalted butter, softened
2	cups [500 mL] icing sugar
2	tsp. [10 mL] vanilla
2	Tbsp. [30 mL] hot water

1. To prepare the cake: Preheat oven to 350°F [180°C] and grease two 9" [23 cm] round metal cake pans. Line pans with parchment paper; set aside.

2. In a medium bowl, whisk together milk, eggs and vanilla; set aside. Sift together flour, sugar, baking powder and salt; set aside. Using an electric mixer, beat butter until creamy, about 2 minutes, scraping down sides of bowl.

3. Alternately add egg mixture and flour mixture, beginning and ending with flour, beating 30 seconds after each addition. Stir in vanilla bean seeds, if using.

4. Pour and scrape batter into prepared pans, smoothing the tops with a spatula. Bake cakes in centre of oven 30-40 minutes or until golden and a toothpick inserted into the cakes comes out clean. Allow to cool in the pans 20 minutes.

5. Unmould onto a cooling rack and peel off parchment paper. Carefully reinvert the cakes onto the racks and allow to cool completely.

6. To prepare the curd: In a large saucepan, combine cranberries and water; cover and cook over medium heat until cranberries have popped, about 5 minutes.

7. Push cranberries through a sieve and return purée to the saucepan. Over low heat, stir in butter and sugar and cook until butter has melted and sugar is beginning to dissolve.

8. In a small bowl, thoroughly beat the eggs, strain them over cranberry mixture and increase heat to medium. Cook mixture, stirring constantly, until thickened about 5 minutes. Allow to cool, then refrigerate, tightly covered, until ready to use.

9. To make icing: In a medium bowl, beat butter with an electric mixer until light and fluffy, about 3 minutes. Gradually beat in icing sugar and vanilla; continue beating until very light and creamy, 2-3 minutes. Slowly add hot water; beat 1 more minute. Set aside, covered, until ready to use.

10. To assemble the cake, place one cake layer bottom side up on a cake plate. Slide strips of waxed paper between cake and plate. Spread cake evenly with cranberry curd.

11. Place second cake layer bottom side up on top of cranberry filling; press down gently on cake. Spread a layer of icing over top and sides of the cake and then finish icing the cake using a spatula to make billowing swirls. Remove waxed paper strips. Serve immediately or cover loosely and refrigerate for up to 2 days. Allow cake to come to room temperature before serving.

Calories: 915; Protein 6.7 g; Carbohydrate 112.2 g; Fibre 0.9 g; Fat 50 g/serving

classic pavlova

MAKES 6 TO 8 SERVINGS

4	egg whites
1/8	tsp. [0.5 mL] cream of tartar
1/2	cup [125 mL] granulated sugar
1/2	cup [125 mL] icing sugar
1	Tbsp. [15 mL] cornstarch
1	tsp. [5 mL] white vinegar

Topping:

1	cup [250 mL] whipping cream
1/2	tsp. [3 mL] vanilla
1	Tbsp. [15 mL] icing sugar
	Assorted fresh or canned fruit, sliced [strawberries, kiwis, etc.]

Calories: 235;
Protein 3 g;
Carbohydrate 32 g;
Fibre 0 g;
Fat 11 g/serving

1. Preheat oven to 325°F [160°C]. Line a baking sheet with parchment paper. Draw an 8"-10" [20-25 cm] circle on the paper. Alternatively, prepare an 8"-10" [20-25 cm] spring-form pan by lining the bottom and sides with parchment paper. Set aside.

2. Place egg whites and cream of tartar in a clean mixing bowl. Be sure there is no trace of any egg yolk, as this will affect the volume of the egg whites. Beat egg whites at high speed until stiff, foamy peaks form.

3. Combine sugars in separate small bowl. Add half of the sugar mixture to the egg whites. Beat until sugar is dissolved. Continue adding sugar 1 Tbsp. [15 mL] at a time, beating well after each addition. Once all the sugars have been added, beat for 1 more minute to ensure all sugar is fully incorporated and dissolved. The meringue mixture will have stiff, glossy peaks at this point.

4. Sprinkle cornstarch and vinegar over mixture. Gently fold in, being careful not to lose any volume.

5. Spoon mixture onto the circle drawn on the prepared baking sheet or springform pan. With the back of the spoon, spread mixture evenly and with a swirling motion. Build up the sides slightly to form a small well in the middle. Bake for 15 minutes.

6. Reduce heat to 250°F [120°C] and continue baking for 1 to 1-1/4 hours. The lower temperature will keep the meringue white to light golden in colour and minimize crack-ing. The meringue is done when it is hard and crunchy when tapped on the outside. A skewer inserted in the middle will find a slightly chewy but dry texture inside. Do not overbake. Remove meringue from oven and allow to cool.

7. Once cooled, gently remove from springform pan or baking sheet. Transfer it directly to the plate or platter you will be serving it on. The meringue can be covered with plastic wrap and stored for up to two days before using.

8. To serve, beat cream with vanilla and icing sugar until stiff peaks form. Spoon whipped cream into the centre of the meringue. Arrange sliced fruit on top. Slice into wedges.

tiramisu

MAKES 12 SERVINGS

1	[500 g] tub Mascarpone cheese
1	cup [250 mL] no-fat sour cream
3/4	cup [175 mL] packed golden sugar
3	Tbsp. [45 mL] cocoa powder
1-1/4	cups [310 mL] very strong espresso coffee, divided
2/3	cup [150 mL] dark rum, divided
1	cup [250 mL] whipping cream
2	Tbsp. [30 mL] granulated sugar
1	white or yellow cake mix [for a double-layer cake]
	Espresso powder
	Cocoa powder
	Chopped semi-sweet chocolate

1. Prepare the cake mix according to package directions in 9" [23 cm] cake pans; cool completely. Alternatively, purchase two prepared 9" [23 cm] sponge cakes.
2. Assemble and pre-measure all the required ingredients. Combine the first 4 ingredients in a large bowl.
3. Mix together the strong coffee and rum. Beat the cheese mixture with an electric mixer, adding 1/2 cup [125 mL] of the coffee/rum mixture as you beat.
4. Clean beaters before beating the whipping cream in a small bowl until nearly stiff; beat in sugar at the end, beating until stiff. Fold the whipped cream into the cheese mixture.
5. Slice each of the cake layers in half, horizontally to produce 4 layers. Place the first one, cut-side up, in the bottom of a 9" [23 cm] springform pan with high sides. Brush with 1/4 of the remaining strong coffee/rum mixture.
6. Spread 1/4 of the cheese mixture over top. Repeat with the remaining 3 layers, always placing the cut side up.
7. Smooth the last cheese layer across the top; wrap in plastic wrap and refrigerate overnight.
8. Sprinkle with espresso powder and/or cocoa powder and chopped chocolate before cutting.

Trifle-Style Tiramisu: It's easy to prepare Tiramisu as a trifle instead of a cake. Simply cube one cake layer and toss with the coffee and rum mixture. Then alternate layers of these soaked cubes with the cheese mixture – either in a large glass bowl or in individual dessert glasses.

Alternative suggestions: Instead of preparing the cake mix, try substituting purchased ladyfingers or sponge cake layers.

Calories 519;
Protein 8 g;
Carbohydrate 54 g;
Fibre 0 g;
Fat 27 g/serving
of cake

pumpkin cheesecake with a gingersnap crust
MAKES 10 TO 12 SERVINGS

Gingersnap Crust:

15-20	gingersnap cookies, processed into crumbs
1/3	cup [75 mL] melted butter

Pumpkin Cheesecake:

12	oz. [360 g] softened cream cheese
1/4	cup [60 mL] granulated sugar
3/4	cup [175 mL] whipping cream
1/2	cup [125 mL] sour cream
1	egg
1	egg yolk
1/2	tsp. [3 mL] vanilla
1	[398 mL] tin pumpkin purée
1/3	cup [75 mL] packed brown sugar
1	tsp. [5 mL] ground cinnamon
1/2	tsp. [3 mL] ground ginger
1/2	tsp. [3 mL] ground cloves

Calories: 488;
Protein 8 g;
Carbohydrate 53 g;
Fibre 1.4 g;
Fat 28 g/serving

1. To prepare crust: Preheat oven to 350°F [180°C]. Combine the gingersnap crumbs with the melted butter.

2. Press crumbs into the bottom of an 8"-10" [20-25 cm] springform pan. Bake in a 350°F [180°C] oven for 10 minutes to set crust. Set aside to cool.

3. To prepare cheesecake: Preheat oven to 250°F [120°C]. In a large mixing bowl, beat cream cheese until smooth. Scrape bowl. Beat again to ensure there are no lumps.

4. Add sugar, whipping cream and sour cream. Beat well and scrape bowl. Add egg, egg yolk and vanilla. Scrape bowl. Mixture should be very smooth at this point.

5. Mix in pumpkin purée, brown sugar and spices just until combined.

6. Pour batter over cooled gingersnap crust. Place in oven and bake 1-1/2 to 2 hours. Cheesecake is done when the centre is set but jiggles slightly and when the cake begins to pull away from the sides of the pan. Cool to room temperature before refrigerating.

7. Chill thoroughly before slicing. To slice, use a sharp knife dipped in hot water and wiped dry.

summer strawberry mousse cake

MAKES 8-10 SERVINGS

Sponge Cake:
6	eggs
1/2	cup [125 mL] granulated sugar
1	tsp. [5 mL] vanilla
2/3	cup [150 mL] all-purpose flour
1/3	cup [75 mL] cake flour
	Pinch salt

Mousse:
1-1/2	tsp. [8 mL] plain gelatin
2	Tbsp. [30 mL] cold water
2-1/2	cups [625 mL] strawberries, cleaned, hulled
3/4	cup [175 mL] granulated sugar
3	Tbsp. [45 mL] freshly squeezed orange juice
1/2	cup [125 mL] Mascarpone cheese, at room temperature
2	cups [500 mL] whipping cream, chilled

1. To prepare the cake: Preheat oven to 350°F [180°C]. Lightly butter the bottom of two 8" [20 cm] round pans and line bottoms with parchment paper. Set aside.
2. In a large bowl, using an electric mixer at medium speed, whisk together the eggs and sugar to combine. Add the vanilla and continue beating until the mixture has tripled in volume and is thick, about 4 minutes.
3. Sift half of the flour and salt over batter and whisk to mix well. Gently fold in the remaining flour, quickly but thoroughly.
4. Divide batter between the pans and spread evenly with a spatula. Bake 20-25 minutes or until tops spring back when lightly pressed. Allow cakes to cool in pans for 5 minutes. Invert onto a cooling rack, peel off parchment and cool completely.
5. Meanwhile, make the mousse. In a small saucepan, sprinkle the gelatin over the cold water and allow to stand for 5 minutes or until gelatin is dissolved.
6. Thinly slice the strawberries and place in a medium saucepan. Add sugar and orange juice; bring to a boil, stirring. Reduce heat to medium and cook for about 10 minutes, stirring occasionally until berries are very soft and mixture has thickened slightly. Remove 1/3 cup [75 mL] of the syrup from the pan and set aside.
7. Warm the gelatin over low heat until dissolved and mixture is smooth. Whisk the gelatin into the strawberry mixture and allow to cool completely.
8. Whip together the Mascarpone and whipping cream until thick. Add the strawberry mixture to the whipped cream and mix well to combine.
9. To assemble the cake: place 1 cake layer on a serving plate. Using a pastry brush, soak the top of the cake with half the reserved syrup. Spread about 1/3 of the mousse over the cake and top with the second cake layer. Soak the top of the cake with the remaining syrup and spread the mousse over the top and sides of the cake. Garnish with whole strawberries and chill for at least 2 hours before serving. The cake can be made 1 day ahead if stored well-wrapped in the refrigerator.

Calories: 445; Protein 8.7 g; Carbohydrate 45 g; Fibre 1.4 g; Fat 26 g/serving

heirloom chocolate cake

MAKES 12 TO 14 SERVINGS

Cake:

3	oz. [90 g] semisweet chocolate, finely chopped
3/4	cup [175 mL] unsalted butter, cubed
1-1/2	cups [375 mL] hot brewed coffee
1	cup [250 mL] loosely packed brown sugar
1	cup [250 mL] granulated sugar
1-1/4	cups [310 mL] all-purpose flour
1-1/4	cups [310 mL] cake flour
1-1/2	cups [375 mL] unsweetened cocoa powder
2	tsp. [10 mL] baking soda
3/4	tsp. [4 mL] baking powder
3/4	tsp. [4 mL] salt
3	eggs
1-1/2	cups [375 mL] regular buttermilk
1	tsp. [5 mL] vanilla

Frosting:

7	oz. [210 g] bittersweet chocolate
1-1/2	cups [375 mL] unsalted butter, softened
1-1/4	cups [310 mL] icing sugar
1	Tbsp. [15 mL] vanilla

*Calories: 643;
Protein 7.3 g;
Carbohydrate 73.7 g;
Fibre 0.4 g;
Fat 39.8 g/serving*

1. Preheat the oven to 350°F [180°C]. Grease two 10" [25 cm] round cake pans. Line pans with parchment paper; grease the paper. Set aside.

2. In a medium bowl, combine the chopped chocolate, cubed butter and hot coffee. Allow mixture to stand, stirring occasionally, until chocolate is melted and smooth.

3. Into a large bowl sift together the brown and granulated sugars, both flours, cocoa powder, baking soda, baking powder and salt; set aside.

4. In another large bowl, using an electric mixer, whip the eggs until thickened [about 3 minutes]. Slowly add buttermilk, vanilla and melted chocolate mixture to eggs, mixing until well combined.

5. Add the sugar/flour mixture and mix on medium speed until well combined. Divide the batter between the prepared pans and bake 40-45 minutes. The cakes are done when a toothpick inserted into the centre comes out clean. Allow to cool for 20 minutes in the pans. Remove from the pans, peel off the parchment and allow the cakes to cool completely on a wire rack.

6. To prepare the frosting: Melt the chocolate over simmering water or in a microwave on low for 2-3 minutes, stirring until smooth. Cool chocolate to room temperature. Using an electric mixer with a whisk attachment, beat melted chocolate with the butter until light and fluffy. Gradually whisk in icing sugar and vanilla; continue beating until light and creamy, about 3-4 minutes.

7. Centre one of the cake layers on a cake plate. Spread a layer of frosting over the cake. Place the second cake layer on top and spread the remaining frosting over the entire cake in billowing swirls. Allow to set for about 45 minutes before serving.

heirloom
chocolate
cake

mango
pudding

mango pudding

MAKES 4 TO 6 SERVINGS

1/2	cup [125 mL] granulated sugar
3/4	cup [175 mL] boiling water
1-1/2	[7 g] pkgs. unflavoured gelatin
1-1/4	cups [310 mL] cold water, divided
1	[30 fl. oz./850 g] tin mango pulp [not pickled in oil]*
1	cup [250 mL] half and half or whipping cream

If you prefer, substitute fresh mango. Choose about 3 very ripe fruit, peel off the skin and cut the flesh into 1/2" [1.25 cm] pieces. You should have about 2 cups [500 mL]. Place the chopped fruit into a food processor and purée until smooth before adding to recipe.

---

1. Dissolve the sugar in boiling water in a large saucepan over medium-low heat.
2. Meanwhile, dissolve gelatin in 3/4 cup [175 mL] cold water, then stir mixture into the sugar water. Mix thoroughly until everything has dissolved. Turn off heat and add the remaining cold water. When the mixture reaches room temperature, mix in the mango pulp and then the cream. Stir well to incorporate.
3. If you prefer a smoother pudding texture pour the mixture through a sieve. Transfer to a serving dish or individual serving dishes and chill overnight or until set. Alternatively, pour into an 8" [20 cm] square cake pan, refrigerate until set and cut into 1-1/2" [3.75 cm] squares to serve.

Calories: 296;
Protein 3 g;
Carbohydrate 37 g;
Fibre 1.7 g;
Fat 16 g/serving

three citrus mousse

MAKES 4 TO 6 SERVINGS

2/3	cup [150 mL] granulated sugar
4	eggs
	Grated peel and juice of 3 lemons*
	Grated peel and juice of 2 limes*
1	envelope unflavoured gelatin
3/4	cup [175 mL] fresh orange juice
1	cup [250 mL] whipping cream
	Extra whipped cream [optional]
	Fresh orange &/or lime segments for decoration [optional]

*If your lemons and limes are very large and juicy, cut the amount of juice slightly.

Calories: 365;
Protein 8 g;
Carbohydrate 36 g;
Fibre 1.2 g;
Fat 21 g/serving

1. In a large saucepan, combine sugar, 2 whole eggs, 2 egg yolks, lemon and lime peel and juice; cook over medium heat, stirring constantly, until thickened. Do not let it boil.

2. Meanwhile, soften gelatin in the orange juice. When egg mixture thickens, stir in softened gelatin and orange juice; continue stirring until gelatin is completely dissolved. Refrigerate until thickened to the consistency of unbeaten egg whites.

3. In a small bowl, beat 2 remaining egg whites until stiff. Using same beaters, beat whipping cream in another small bowl until stiff. Fold all three mixtures together gently, leaving lumps of cream showing.

4. Transfer to a serving bowl or dessert/wine glasses. Cover with plastic wrap; refrigerate at least 2 hours. Decorate with more whipped cream and/or fruit segments before serving.

coconut crème brûlée

MAKES 4 SERVINGS

Custard:

1	cup [250 mL] coconut milk*
1	vanilla bean, split
1	cup [250 mL] light cream
3	eggs
1/4	cup [60 mL] granulated sugar

Caramel Topping:

6	Tbsp. [90 mL] packed brown sugar
3	Tbsp. [45 mL] water

Use coconut milk, not coconut cream.

1. Preheat oven to 325°F [160°C].
2. Pour coconut milk into a medium saucepan; add vanilla bean. Gently heat over low heat for about 5 minutes. Do not allow liquid to boil. When coconut milk is hot, remove saucepan from the heat; set aside for 10 minutes to infuse and cool down.
3. Place cream, eggs and sugar in a blender or food processor; blend until smooth.
4. Remove vanilla bean from the cooled coconut milk; add coconut milk to blender or food processor; blend 3-5 seconds.
5. Pour mixture into one deep 8" [20 cm] baking dish or 4 individual ramekins. Stand the dish[es] in a deep baking pan filled with hot water to half the depth of the baking dish or ramekins. Carefully place into centre of the oven. Bake until custard is cooked through and firm to the touch, about 30-40 minutes if using individual dishes, or 1 hour if using a large baking dish.
6. When cooked, remove custards from the oven; cool to room temperature, then cover with plastic wrap and refrigerate overnight.
7. To serve, remove dishes from refrigerator.
8. Make topping by placing brown sugar and water in a small saucepan over medium heat. Bring to the boil; continue to stir until sugar dissolves and mixture turns pale golden – about 5-7 minutes. Work very quickly to pour small amounts of the caramel over the top of each custard.
9. Refrigerate for another 2-3 hours before serving.

Calories: 403;
Protein 7.5 g;
Carbohydrate 36.9 g;
Fibre 0 g;
Fat 26.6 g/serving

PHOTO: JOHN SINAL

three-tiered chocolate mousse

MAKES 6 TO 8 SERVINGS

3   oz. [90 g] white chocolate, finely chopped
3   oz. [90 g] milk chocolate, finely chopped
3   oz. [90 g] bittersweet chocolate, finely chopped
3   Tbsp. [45 mL] unsalted butter
3   cups [750 mL] whipping cream, chilled, divided

Calories: 518;
Protein 3.9 g;
Carbohydrate 23.1 g;
Fibre 0 g;
Fat 47.7 g/serving

1. Place each chocolate into a separate medium mixing bowl.

2. Add 1 Tbsp. [15 mL] of butter to each bowl.

3. Divide 1 cup [250 mL] of the cream between the 3 bowls.

4. Place each bowl in the microwave and heat on high for 2 minutes. Whisk each of the mixtures until smooth and creamy. Allow to cool.

5. Meanwhile, whip the remaining 2 cups [500 mL] cream until well thickened, but not overly stiff.

6. Divide the whipped cream between the 3 bowls. Lightly but thoroughly fold the cream into each of the chocolate mixtures.

7. Starting with the bittersweet chocolate, spoon or pipe the mousse into 6 or 8 individual dessert glasses.

8. Continue layering with the milk chocolate and finish with the white.

9. Cover the glasses and refrigerate for at least 6 hours. Garnish with chocolate curls if desired.

iced strawberry swirl soufflé

MAKES 8 SERVINGS

Raspberry Swirl:

2	cups [500 mL] fresh or frozen unsweetened raspberries
1/4	cup [60 mL] granulated sugar

Soufflé:

4	cups [1 L] fresh strawberries, cleaned, hulled
1	cup [250 mL] granulated sugar
1	cup [250 mL] whipping cream
1	tsp. [5 mL] vanilla
3	egg whites
	Pinch salt

1. To make the raspberry swirl: Combine the raspberries and sugar in a small saucepan. Cook the berries over medium-low heat for 12 minutes, stirring and breaking up the berries with the back of a spoon.
2. Force the berries through a fine sieve into a clean bowl. Set aside to cool.
3. Lightly butter a 7 cups [1.75 L] soufflé dish or decorative glass bowl and sprinkle with sugar. Alternatively, line the outside of an 8" [20 cm] high-sided springform pan with aluminum foil.
4. Set aside 8-10 of the prettiest strawberries for garnishing the soufflé and purée the rest with the sugar. Set aside.
5. Whip the cream until it forms soft peaks.
6. In a second bowl, whip the egg whites with the salt until stiff but not dry. Fold the strawberry purée and whipped cream into the beaten whites gently but thoroughly. There should be no streaks remaining. Scrape the mixture into the prepared dish, smoothing the top.
7. Spoon 1/2 of the raspberry purée over the top of the soufflé and swirl lightly with a dull knife.
8. Freeze the soufflé for 6 hours or overnight.
9. To serve: Remove the soufflé from the freezer 20 minutes before serving. Garnish with the reserved strawberries, and serve with the remaining raspberry purée. If using a springform pan, release the sides of the pan and slice the soufflé into 1" [2.5 cm] slices.

Calories: 267;
Protein 2.8 g;
Carbohydrate 42.6 g;
Fibre 3.3 g;
Fat 10.6 g/serving

PHOTO: RAEFF MILES

cantaloupe sorbet

MAKES 3 CUPS [750 ML]

7	oz. [210 mL] granulated sugar
7	oz. [210 mL] water
1/2	ripe cantaloupe, seeded, peeled, diced
1/4	cup [60 mL] fresh lime juice

Calories: 73;
Protein 0.2 g;
Carbohydrate 19 g;
Fibre 0.2 g;
Fat 0.1 g/serving

1. Place sugar and water in a small saucepan and bring to a boil over high heat. Reduce heat and simmer gently for 10 minutes. Remove the syrup from heat and let cool slightly.

2. Meanwhile, in a blender or food processor, purée diced melon. Add the sugar syrup to the puréed melon and stir to combine. Stir in lime juice.

3. Pour mixture into an 8" x 11" [20 x 27.5 cm] baking dish or similar-sized container and place on a flat surface in the freezer. Every half hour, take the sorbet out of the freezer and stir to blend, removing any lumps. Repeat until the mixture is frozen and smooth.

4. Store the sorbet in a covered container in the freezer until ready to use.

Variations:

Watermelon Sorbet: Use about 3 cups [750 mL] diced watermelon instead of the cantaloupe.

Cantaloupe Creamsicles: Use a Popsicle form and fill half way with Cantaloupe Sorbet, pressing it in firmly. Fill the remaining half with vanilla ice cream. You'll need a 1 L container of vanilla ice cream. Insert a Popsicle stick and freeze until firm. Place the form under running warm water to release "Creamsicles."

index